D1389425

SHAGGY DOGS AND
BLACK SHEEP

SHAGGY DOGS AND BLACK SHEEP

The Origins of Even More Phrases We Use Every Day

Albert Jack
Illustrator: Ama Page

PENGUIN BOOKS

PENGUIN BOOKS

Published by the Penguin Group
Penguin Books Ltd, 80 Strand, London WC2R ORL, England
Penguin Group (USA) Inc., 375 Hudson Street, New York, New York 10014, USA
Penguin Group (Canada), 90 Eglinton Avenue East, Suite 700, Toronto, Ontario,
Canada M4P 3YZ (a division of Pearson Penguin Canada Inc.)
Penguin Ireland, 25 St Stephen's Green, Dublin 2, Ireland
(a division of Penguin Books Ltd)
Penguin Group (Australia), 250 Camberwell Road, Camberwell, Victoria 3124,
Australia (a division of Pearson Australia Group Pty Ltd)
Penguin Books India Pvt Ltd, 11 Community Centre,
Panchsheel Park, New Delhi – 110 017, India
Penguin Group (NZ), cnr Airborne and Rosedale Roads, Albany,
Auckland 1310, New Zealand (a division of Pearson New Zealand Ltd)
Penguin Books (South Africa) (Pty) Ltd, 24 Sturdee Avenue,
Rosebank 2196, South Africa

Penguin Books Ltd, Registered Offices: 80 Strand, London WC2R ORL, England

www.penguin.com

First published 2005
1

Albert Jack supports the MacKinnon Trust, a registered charity working to raise
awareness about mental health issues such as schizophrenia and the care needed
by those who suffer and their families. *www.mackinnontrust.org*

Albert Jack's website is *www.albertjack.com*

The moral right of the author has been asserted

Set in 11.5/14pt Adobe Minion
Typeset by Palimpsest Book Production Limited, Polmont, Stirlingshire
Printed in England by Clays Ltd, St Ives plc

This book is dedicated to the Fathers 4 Justice movement. There are far too many people who believe that to crowbar one loving parent out of their own children's lives is either a good thing or acceptable. It never is.

Reading Instructions: Place beside toilet – open when seated.

CONTENTS

CONTENTS

ACKNOWLEDGEMENTS

Thanks in the first place to Lance Rossouw and all the staff at the Gaborone Sun Hotel in Botswana who made my stay both enjoyable and productive. After all, that was where this book was written. Thanks too to many good people in Botswana for their warm welcome and hospitality, to Greg Powell in Cape Town, and to my sister Julie Willmott and her kids Sam and Faye for coming out and keeping me company for a while.

Special thanks also to my agent Robert Smith for all the good work, Georgina Laycock, Ellie Smith and Andrew Henty at Penguin Books and my copy-editor Kate Parker. As usual, Peter Gordon has to get a mention, though I can't think of any decent reason this time, and the same goes for Peter Patsalides, Paul Ryan, Tony Henderson, Joe Hobbs, Andy Ellis (for the website) and Martyn Long for the hangover that provided the initial inspiration for the two books.

Then there are those that helped along the way: Philip Schofield, Fern Britton and the crew at ITV's *This Morning*, Andy McDaniel and Denise Hance, Dee Muldoon, Paul March of Clintons (the lawyers), Dennis Hill and Olivia Hill.

And, last but not least, I would like to thank all the enthusiastic readers of *Red Herrings and White Elephants* for their suggestions, especially John Davey, Bruce Wilson, Philomena Jacques, Henry Lally and Tom Fattorini. I received thousands of emails, far more than I could ever properly reply to, so please do accept my sincere thanks here rather than in person. I read and appreciated every one.

INTRODUCTION

The expressions that litter the English language have long fascinated me. And I'm not alone in this. While researching my last book, *Red Herrings and White Elephants*, I began to think it might well prove popular, if the conversations I was having at the time were anything to go by. Like most, these were peppered with the strange idioms we all use every day without thinking. Now I had tuned in to them, they stuck out like a series of sore thumbs.

I soon became notorious for my constant interruptions, wondering where a particular expression comes from and why we use it. This had the unfortunate side-effect of my not being invited to many dinner parties any more because if I was there the conversation tended to veer, often for hours, between why there should be 'more than one way to skin a cat' to discussing who was 'dressed up to the nines' or, if I was feeling brave enough, 'looking like a dog's dinner'.

One of the first questions people always ask me is: 'How do you go about researching the origins of all of those expressions?' I am often tempted to reply that it takes months of painstaking cutting and pasting from the internet to produce a book like this. The research took a fair bit of time, it's true, but it turned out to be the most rewarding part of the process.

The hardest part was to think of a phrase in the first place. There are probably over two thousand idioms we all use on a regular basis and yet when you sit down and try to think up a few dozen, it is almost impossible. I have discovered that the best way is to consciously listen out for them. However, don't try this at home. I haven't had a conversation, read a book, or watched TV without a notebook to hand for over two years now.

Researching this book, I have waded through thousands of bizarre treatises, reference books and English histories in many libraries. Most notably I have been lucky enough to have access to the libraries of the Houses of Commons and of Lords, which have provided many answers. And the material has come from many other unexpected places such as, for example, George Orwell's social commentary *Down and Out in Paris and London*, which has inadvertently provided illuminating examples of some popular idioms in action (see, for instance, **Sleep on a Clothes Line** and **Toe-rag**).

This time round I decided to research single words as well as phrases. And I was soon **Mesmerized** by the hashish-smoking **Assassins**, the activities of the **Lynch Mob**, what the **Cakewalk** was all about and what a **Toady** got up to. Along the way I discovered fascinating stories behind some good old expressions such as to **Bell the Cat** and **Apply Morton's Fork**, which hopefully might now make a comeback. (See what you think.)

As with *Red Herrings* the idea was not to provide a definitive English-language guide but to choose the words and phrases with the most interesting origins. That is why you won't find expressions like 'as tough as old boots' or 'as alike as two peas in a pod' in here because the origins of these are obvious. But if you are hoping to **Butter Someone Up** after you have found yourself **Drinking at the Last Chance Saloon**, then try giving them *Shaggy Dogs and Black Sheep*. **A Little Bird Tells Me** that **Before You Can Say Jack Robinson**, you might just become the **Bee's Knees** once more.

Albert Jack, Cape Town, July 2005

www.albertjack.com

MONEY (OR THE LACK OF IT)

To **Blackmail** somebody is to demand money by threats, usually to expose secrets. This word originated from the Highlands of Scotland in the 1600s. The 'mail' in blackmail is the old Scottish word for 'rent', usually spelt either *maill* or *male,* which in turn evolved from the Old Norse word *mal,* meaning 'agreement' or 'contract'. In those days, tenants paid their rent in silver coins, which used to be known as 'white money', but in the 17th century the chiefs of the Highland clans began a protection racket threatening farmers and traders with violence if they didn't pay to be protected from other clans. This informal tax, or additional rent, soon became known as 'black money' or 'black rent', being the opposite of white rent. Hence 'blackmail' became part of the English language as a word used to describe the practice of obtaining money by threat of violence.

Those unable to pay would have their stock confiscated and this would then be sold on the **Black Market**.

There is another suggestion for the origin of the expression **Black Market**. Centuries earlier, in medieval England, mercenaries and freelancers would travel the country and sell their fighting skills to the lords and noblemen who were raising armies. They were hardened soldiers who lived rough for most of the time and, subjected to the elements and seldom polished, consequently their armour often oxidized into a blackish colour. These men became known as the Black Knights. Sometimes, at the local festivals, they would take part in jousting exhibitions and the victor would win his opponent's weapons and armour. The Black Knights usually triumphed, but rather than carry around extra sets of armour, they would sell them locally on what became known as the 'black market'. Take your pick, but I feel the Scottish origin is the most likely source.

To be **Dressed Up to the Nines** means to be wearing our finest suit or evening gown. Some suggestions for the origin of this phrase lead us to tailoring and the belief that it takes nine yards of material to make the perfect three-piece suit. But that seemed a little bit weak to me, so I looked further and found most sources insist it began as 'dressed up to the eyes', which has been corrupted over the years. Still not convinced, I decided to work backwards and look for all the possible uses of the word 'nine', discovering a little gem in the process. In the precious metals industry, the finest gold and silver are never classified as 100 per cent pure, but as 99.99 per cent; hence the finest metals are known as 'the nines'. It is my belief that 'being dressed up in your nines' means to be wearing your finest jewellery. Further evidence to support this theory lies in the archive of the Royal Gloucester, Berkshire and Wiltshire Regimental Museum in Salisbury. Queen Victoria's favourite regiment was the Wiltshire (Duke of Edinburgh's) 99th Foot. Stationed at Aldershot, they were always chosen to guard the Royal Pavilion in Brighton, consequently becoming known as 'the Queen's Pets'. The officers' dress code included an unusual amount of gold lace on their uniforms; hence they were regarded as being 'dressed up in their nines' for royal duty.

To be **Taken to the Cleaners** means you have been the victim of a con and, as a result, lost most or all of your money. During the 1800s, the expression 'to be cleaned out' was in regular use to explain a situation where a person had been 'stripped clean' or 'cleaned' of their possessions, either by fraud or as a result of gambling losses. The phrase changed slightly during the 20th century with the introduction of dry cleaners, and from then on any careless person could be 'taken there'.

*

To **Apply Morton's Fork** is a phrase that was used for centuries to describe a situation where a person has no choice whatsoever. Very few people know the expression these days as the American equivalent (see **Catch-22**) has largely replaced it, but it is about time it made a comeback and we started to use it again on this side of the pond. During the late 15th century (long before Joseph Heller wrote *Catch-22*) John Morton (1420–1500) was the Archbishop of Canterbury and a minister in Henry VII's government. His job was to raise money for the king in the name of 'loans' from the English nobility, and he used what he called his 'fork' as a method of finding out if a person had spare money to lend the king. It went something like this: Morton claimed that if a person looked obviously rich, then they would have enough money to loan to the king. If, on the other hand, they appeared outwardly poor, then Morton reasoned they were not spending their wealth on themselves and were probably hiding something from him. Such folk must have money stashed away and therefore (you guessed it) would have enough hidden wealth to give money to King Henry. God help those who didn't pay up.

If something is offered for sale as **Cheap at Half the Price** it is being sold as a bargain. Many people have been baffled by this sales tactic, and with good reason too. 'If it would be cheap at half of this price, then make it half of this price instead of suggesting it is expensive at this price, and then I might buy it,' they might say. Some go even further and claim the phrase should be 'cheap at twice the price', meaning it would still be a bargain if the price were doubled. But all of that is to miss the point completely.

During the Second World War, when basic items were hard to obtain and inflation was causing problems for everybody, many shops could charge whatever they liked for everyday goods such as food, clothing and toiletries. However, street traders and market stallholders were usually able to offer the same items for sale at half of the price listed in the major stores. This led to their advertising slogans and signboards offering goods cheaply and at 'half of the price a buyer might expect to pay elsewhere'. We only need to re-word the phrase slightly to understand their meaning. 'Being sold cheaply here at half the price you will pay anywhere else' would have prevented any confusion in our understanding of the phrase today. But it doesn't trip off the tongue in quite the same way, does it?

A **Skinflint** is a miserly person, who has deep pockets and short arms. He, or she, doesn't readily pay for anything if it can possibly be avoided. Skinflints are not poor people, they are just mean. In the old days, the term 'to skin a flint' was used to describe driving a hard bargain, or making a tight deal. Similar terms used to exist, such as the Latin phrase *lana caprina* ('goat's wool') and 'the fleece of an egg'. Goats don't have wool, of course, and eggs have no fleece. Each are as meaningless as the skin of a flint (a flintstone has no skin), but of the three of them only the word 'skinflint' seems to have survived, meaning somebody who would gather and keep worthless items, yet be reluctant to let go of them (i.e. miserly).

To call a person a **Toe-rag** is mildly offensive, although these days it is considered cheeky rather than insulting. The first recorded use dates back to 1875 and a book called *Experiences of a Convict* (1864) by J. F. Mortlock, who states: 'Stockings are unknown, so some luxurious men wrapped round their feet a piece of old shirting, called, in language more expressive than elegant, a "toe-rag".' By 'stockings' Mortlock means 'socks', which had been a luxury that vagrants and tramps, for centuries prior to that, were unable to afford. Instead, to avoid the discomfort of wearing worn-out old boots next to their skin, they would tear strips of cloth from the tails of their old shirts and wrap them around their feet, in place of socks. Often these were the only items of clothing a person in this situation would ever wash. George Orwell brought this practice to wider public knowledge in *Down and Out in Paris and London* (1933): 'Less than half the tramps actually bathed (I heard them say that hot water is "weakening" to the system, but they all washed their faces and feet, and the horrid greasy little clouts known as toe-rags which they bind around their toes.' This was quickly picked up and used in cockney rhyming slang to describe a 'slag' (convict or lag). In the 1970s, the London-based police series *The Sweeney* regularly used the phrase 'toe-rag' to describe a trouble-maker. In fact, this popular programme often used rhyming slang throughout. Even the title derives from 'Sweeney Todd (flying squad)'.

The quaint old English expression **That's Just the Ticket** means 'just what I needed and at just the right time'. Some believe the phrase derives from a corruption of the French word *étiquette*. The idea is that the right way to proceed comes from 'eti-quette', or the formal procedures and customs that ensure matters run smoothly. But there is another, more likely, suggestion dating back to before the Second World War when 'meal tickets' were handed out to the needy in exchange for essential items such as food and clothing. During and after the war, ration books were distributed and it is easy to imagine a shopkeeper exclaiming, 'That's the ticket!' when the correct one was produced for a certain transaction. The French word *étiquette* can also be translated as 'ticket'; hence 'that's the ticket' actually means 'that's the right etiquette' across the Channel.

To be **Stony Broke** means to be hard up, out of cash or near financial ruin. This expression was in reg-ular use by 1886 and reminds us of the darker side of the great Victorian empire when craftsmen and skilled workers, finding themselves in debt, would have their tools repossessed and their stone benches broken up if they failed to make repayments. They also used to send such poor wretches to debtors' prison where they could be sentenced for up to two years, with repeat offenders being given hard labour (breaking rocks or stones). I wonder why they just didn't cut their hands off and make it impossible for them to work ever again to repay their debts.

Someone who is **Browned Off** is not a happy person and is extremely fed up with a situation. According to some research, this expression has its roots in the colourful London slang from between the two World Wars. In those days, the slang word for a penny piece was a 'brown', and if a person was annoying someone in any way, particularly on the street, they might be given a penny and simply told to go away. The recipient of the coin had thus been 'browned off', which gives the phrase we use today the hint of rejection it has about it.

During the first half of the 20th century, small coins were pressed out of a hard-wearing nickel-brass alloy, which is how the term **Brassed Off** became used as an alternative to 'browned off'. And this is where the word **Nickel**, used in America for a coin of small value, comes from. In Britain, the coin of least value, also made out of a brass alloy, used to be the farthing. This led to the expression 'without even a brass farthing' being used to indicate poverty. In his book *Naaman the Syrian, His Disease and Cure* (1642), Daniel Rogers includes the line: 'As bare and beggarly as if he had not one brasse farthing'. Meanwhile, two centuries later, Sir Walter Besant and James Rice used 'I care not one brass farthing' in their novel *The Seamy Side* (1880).

When everything ends up **Even Stevens** it means it has been divided up equally. This could refer to the result of a sports match or the way a financial reward has been shared out. Jonathan Swift wrote in his *Journal to Stella* (1748): 'Now we are even, quoth Stephen, when he gave his wife six blows for one.' But the origin of the expression is much more likely to derive from the Dutch word *stuiver*, meaning 'small money' or something of little value. In the early 1700s there was certainly a low-value coin circulating the Cape, which was under the influence of the Dutch East India Trading Company, and it is also known that in England, at around that time, the slang word for coins was 'stevens'. During the 1800s, associated expressions came about, such as 'Steven is at home', meaning a person had funds. In the circumstances, it would appear the phrase arose thanks to a simple piece of rhyming slang.

When a business venture has **Gone South**, it has failed completely and the investment has been lost.

The South Sea Scheme, also known as the South Sea Bubble, was a stock investment plan dreamt up by Sir John Blunt between 1710 and 1720. The idea was to buy out the British national debt by encouraging investors to pay £100 per share for a stake in a South Seas trading company. No sooner had they been issued than the shares increased ten times in value, but in 1720 the share scheme famously collapsed, bringing financial ruin on thousands of people in the process. This is also the source of the expression **The Bubble Has Burst.**

To **Have No Truck** with a person or a situation is to avoid them completely and have no dealings at all with them, especially in business matters. The root of this expression is the Old French word *troquer*, meaning 'to barter'. There was a time, centuries ago, when employees in England would be paid all or part of their wages by what was known then as the Troquer System. Instead of being given hard cash, workers would receive goods, tokens or other items that they could trade or exchange. It was a traditional bartering method, but, as it was open to corruption, the government introduced a series of measures throughout the 19th century that effectively put an end to the practice. This was mainly because, by then, many workers were refusing to 'have any truck', meaning they would not work with employers who imposed the Troquer System.

*

Whoever is **Holding the Purse Strings** is the one in control of the budget and financial spending, either in a household, a business or in government. Originally, purses were leather pouches drawn closed at the top by a string. This was often then hung around a person's neck or tied to a belt around the waist. The person who had the money pouch tied to them was, quite literally, holding the purse strings.

A **Lame Duck** is a person (or venture) with no influence and no future, having been incapacitated by misfortune, perhaps of their own making. The expression has been in use since 1761 and is said to have been applied to a defaulter on the London Stock Exchange who could not pay his debts and would have to 'waddle' out of Exchange Alley in the City of London in disgrace. However, the expression became widely used after the publication of William Thackeray's *Vanity Fair* (1847–8), in which the ambitious Mr Osborne, doubtful about the financial security of Amelia's father, states: 'I will have no lame duck's daughter in my family.'

'I could **Sleep on a Clothes Line**' is something we might say when we are so tired that we could sleep anywhere at all. Many people believe this naturally relates to the idea that an exhausted person can even sleep pegged on to a clothes line, untroubled by the idea they might fall off. But there is, in fact, a proper explanation. Although the Victorian era produced great wealth for some, many families still lived in poverty and thousands were forced to sleep rough in towns and villages across the land. In the mid 19th century, workhouses, doss houses and other cheap forms of accommodation began to spring up and these were usually dirty, overcrowded and very uncomfortable. The cheapest of all were the lodge houses, which were so cramped inside that people had to sleep sitting on a long bench, wedged in next

to each other. As even the most dog tired still may have had trouble sleeping in an upright position, lodge owners would string a penny rope (clothes line) along the front of them at chest height, stretch it tight and folk could then spend the night slumped over that. Early the following morning, the clothes line would be cut or untied, waking the guests as they all crashed to the floor in front of them. George Orwell describes one of these lodgings, known as 'Twopenny Hangovers', in his book *Down and Out in Paris and London* (1933): 'At the Twopenny Hangover, the lodgers sit in a row on a bench; there is a rope in front of them, and they lean on this as though leaning over a fence. A man, humorously called the valet, cuts the rope at five in the morning. Apparently they are more comfortable than they sound.'

To **Make Ends Meet** is to live frugally, just about within your means. In this context, the word 'meet' is an early accounting term meaning 'to match' or 'to balance', in other words make the income column match the expenses column on an accounting sheet so that the ends of each column (i.e. the total sum in each case) match each other ('meet') and the accounts balance. The first reference to the expression in print can be found in 1662 when Thomas Fuller wrote of Cumberland: 'Worldly wealth he cared not for, desiring only to make both ends [of his balance sheet] meet.' Nearly 90 years later, the phrase was clearly in common use, as we find in Tobias Smollett's *Roderick Random* (1748): 'He made shift to make the two ends of the year meet.'

To **Stump Up a Payment** means to make a payment, or hand over money, sooner rather than later. 'Stumpy' was the slang word for money during the 1800s, and 'to stumpy up' or 'stump up' was a regularly used phrase for paying rent or other bills that were due immediately.

*

A **Tip** can be either a small extra payment to show gratitude for good service or a piece of exclusive information and advice. In *Believe it or Not* (1928), a collection of linguistic curiosities, the author, J. R. Ripley, suggests the word is an acronym for 'To Insure Promptness' and that the payment should be made at the start of the evening, not at the end. This is the way I always tip waiters and bar staff and it usually works very well. In regular use in England since the 1600s, the word is probably Scandinavian in origin where it once meant 'to fall over' (which is where the expression 'tipsy' comes from). The word has also been used to mean 'to hand or pass over', which is more likely to be the original source of the term. This is also how we find the origin of 'tip' in the sense of 'to pass, or to hand over' advice in order to give a person an advantage, usually in a business or sporting context.

When something is **Up to the Mark** it is acceptable to us; when it is **Not Up to the Mark** it is unacceptable. The 'mark' is seen as a recognized standard, and that is exactly what it was initially. Since 1697, when the Britannia standard was introduced, all gold and silver has been stamped with a 'hallmark' by the assay office to prove its authenticity. All precious metals, where the purity satisfied the examiner, would receive a hallmark as a sign to buyers and jewellers that the metal was genuine. Any falling short of the required standard was rejected as 'not up to the hallmark'. At first, all precious metals were inspected at Goldsmiths Hall in London, and it was the Goldsmiths hallmark that buyers would be looking to see stamped in the surface. Over time this inspection process was carried out in varying locations, so the 'Goldsmiths' part of the term was subsequently dropped, and the idiom 'up to the hallmark' was eventually shortened to the more familiar 'up to the mark'.

ALL AT SEA

When you give a person, or perhaps a situation, a **Wide Berth** you are avoiding them at some distance. At sea a berth is the place in which a ship drops anchor, and berths are allocated to all boats in a harbour. But any boat, large or small, will float around on the tide in any direction, to the limit of its anchor rope. Therefore when anchoring your vessel for the night, it would be wise to give the other boats in the harbour a wide berth lest they move on the tide and collide with yours.

Someone who is **Footloose and Fancy Free** is regarded as single and able to enjoy themselves by flitting around from one place to another without any responsibility to another person. The 'foot' here is the bottom part of the sail on a boat; if this became detached from the boom, the lower half of the sail was regarded as 'footloose' as it flapped around aimlessly in the wind ('fancy free'). The expression has been in regular use since the 18th century to describe single people having fun (probably not at sea, though).

To be caught between the **Devil and the Deep Blue Sea** is not advisable as there is no easy way out. On board the traditional wooden ships, sailors would regularly have to seal the seams between planks with hot tar to prevent them from leaking. The 'devil' seam was the highest one adjacent to the waterways (or gutters) closest to the side of the ship. This was the longest seam on a boat and the most prone to leaking, so inevitably needed the most attention. In heavy seas or during battle, a sailor may slip, or be knocked, into the seam and find himself trapped halfway down the side of the ship, between the devil seam and the 'deep blue sea'. And that was no place to find yourself in at all.

When we get a new job, we are quite often assigned to a person who **Knows the Ropes**, so we can learn from them. This is a simple phrase to explain, as the origin again derives from the old sailing ships of the 17th and 18th centuries. These ships were propelled by vast sails, which were all connected together by an intricate webbing of ropes. The ropes were in constant use as boats changed course, increased their speed, slowed down and navigated their way on both the high seas and in harbour waters. The ropes were just about the most important part of a ship and it took a vastly experienced and capable seaman to understand how they all worked and what they were connected to. Looking at pictures of those old ships, it would be easy to imagine one setting sail for an exotic, far-away location, then end up buried in the harbour wall. Only the most trusted and competent sailor would be assigned to 'learn the ropes' and a true master would then teach them.

Anybody who has ever travelled on the London Underground at rush hour knows what **Choc a Block** feels like. Passengers are rammed in and have nowhere to move. On the sailing ships of days gone by, blocks of rigging tackle would often tangle with

each other and become tightly fixed together. At sea this was known as 'choc a block' and the expression passed from there into wider English usage to describe any tightly packed situation.

When drinking with friends, it is not unusual for someone to announce '**Bottoms Up!**' as the session begins. Many imagine this to be the action of draining a glass so that the bottom is raised higher than our lips. Not so; in fact, events in history once again provide the root of this well-known phrase. During the 18th and 19th centuries, English press gangs would coerce drinkers in London's dockside pubs into joining the armed forces, usually the navy. Men who accepted the 'King's shilling' were deemed to have willingly contracted to join the navy, and this led to unscrupulous behaviour by the commissioned press gangs. One of their dishonest techniques was to drop a shilling into the pint pot of a drunk or unsuspecting man, which would go undetected until the poor chap had drained his tankard. Once the shilling was discovered, the press gangers claimed to others that this was proof a payment had been accepted, and the victim would then be dragged away to wake up the following morning on board a ship far out to sea, unaware of what had happened to him the night before. The unfortunate fellow might then spend years on the ocean wave. Once public houses and drinkers became aware of this scam, they introduced tankards with transparent bases (which can still be found hanging in many pubs to this day) and customers would be reminded to lift the pint up and check the bottom for illicit shillings before they began drinking.

To **Trim Your Sails** is to reduce your spending, and other activities, in line with your present circumstances. The full version of the nautical idiom is to 'trim your sails before the wind'. In heavy weather, sailors will reef the sails when the wind is strong and let them out again in calmer waters. It has a similar meaning to the expression 'to cut your coat according to your cloth'.

A **Reefer** is an early name for a midshipman, so called because of his work reefing sails. The rolled reef of a sail closely resembles a rolled marijuana cigarette, which is how a slang term for a joint became 'reefer'. Very possibly the early sailors and explorers were sometimes a lot higher than just the top of their masts.

The earliest reference to 'colours' as a means of identification can be traced back to the English navy, who adopted the term in 1706 to describe their flags of identity. Since then, we have regularly used expressions containing the term, such as to **Nail One's Colours to the Mast**. We will often hear this said of a person who is resolute in his or her principles or view of events. We might even take it as a public declaration of allegiance. Since 1706, battleships around the world have flown their national ensign proudly from both the mainmast and at other points on the vessel. In times of battle, a flag might be lowered as a sign of surrender, as any ship taking a pounding could lower the main flag and capitulate. But it might not be a captain or senior officer taking that decision. Any frightened sailor, amid the chaos of battle, could loosen the rope and take his chances as a prisoner of the enemy. Let's face it: an able able seaman would simply be put back to work aboard the conquering ship – a considerably better option than a watery end.

To prevent this, dedicated and brave sea captains might order the flag rope to be literally 'nailed' into the mast, preventing any sign of surrender being made during battle. Since the early 18th century, the term has been used to describe a determined or principled person. Sir Robert Peel used the phrase in the *Croker Papers* (1844) when he ridiculed a political opponent: 'I have never heard him (Ashburton) make a speech during the course of which he did not nail, unnail, renail and unnail his colours again.' Arnold Bennett when writing *The Matador of the Five Towns* (1912) included the line: 'She could not conceive in what ignominy the dreadful affairs would end, but she was the kind of woman that nails her colours to the mast.'

By contrast, to **Sail Under False Colours** would suggest we had a scoundrel on our hands. During the 18th and 19th centuries, piracy was a serious problem for the authorities, especially around Britain with its vast network of inlets and coves. Pirate ships would sail along the coastline for months on end looking for one of the many trade ships making its way back to the ports, full of valuable goods imported via England's new trading routes all over the world. Honest and hardworking merchant seamen were likely to risk their lives in faraway lands, then face the dangers of the high seas for several years only to be ambushed by pirates just off the Cornish coast. Lucrative cargoes could be lost for ever, along with many lives. One tactic the pirates successfully adopted was to fly the ensign of a friendly nation, enabling them to get close to an unsuspecting merchant ship before revealing their **True Colours**.

If a situation is **Touch and Go** then it is a very close-run thing. The phrase can be traced to the days of the horse-drawn carriage when there were no rules of etiquette and certainly no highway code. Accidents, collisions and near misses were a common occurrence. In the case of a full-blown collision, matters could become very complicated, as there was no insurance system in those days, few witnesses in the sparsely populated countryside and rarely any way to resolve matters fairly. However, in the case of an accident that was fairly minor, it was usually regarded as 'touch and go', meaning the carriages had barely touched each other, the damage was minor, and the occupants of each carriage could go on their way without repercussion.

A second theory suggests it is a nautical expression referring to when a ship's keel touches the seabed in shallow water, but the vessel is not completely grounded and hence left high and dry. Instead, if the ship is able to move off again, the situation is known as 'touch and go'. The expression to be **Left High and Dry** is used to describe being stranded in a situation without support or resource, and has been in use since the early 1800s (dating from around the time of the Battle of Trafalgar in 1805). The phrase was used to indicate a ship that had been left grounded (possibly it had been 'touch and go' for a while) and then vulnerable to attack as the tide went out. The captain of a ship that had been left 'high and dry' could do nothing to resolve the situation until the tide turned and he could re-float his boat.

*

To be **On Your Beam Ends** is to be virtually destitute; you have run out of cash and had better start making other plans. The beams on the old wooden sailing ships were huge, heavy timbers that ran directly across the vessel, both holding up the deck and butting each side of the hull to prevent it caving inwards. In later years, when these old boats gave way to the steel-hulled ships that Isambard Kingdom Brunel was designing, most of them were broken up and the timbers were salvaged to build new houses. It was these strong beam timbers that builders of the period used in roof voids, which is why they are still called, to this very day, 'roof beams'. So, why was this phrase used to describe being in a perilous position financially? It is recorded that a ship known to be on its beam ends was listing so badly that it was said to be sailing virtually on its side. To be so close to capsizing completely, with such disastrous consequences, was no place to be at all, and neither is being virtually bankrupt – so the parallel was drawn. The phrase quickly travelled back to the land and has been in use ever since. Ships' beams are responsible for another unflattering phrase, as those who are particularly wide in girth are considered to be **Broad in the Beam**, an expression used to describe ladies of a certain size. In fact, there is one who fits the bill sitting directly opposite me as I write, but she will never know I added this line.

*

A **Copper-bottomed** agreement or contract is the safest and most reliable you can have. This is another nautical expression deriving from the copper sheathing ship makers used to strengthen boats, wrapping it around the part of a wooden hull that lies below the water line. This would protect a ship from damage from floating debris, coral reefs, rocks and icebergs, unless, of course, it took a direct hit at **Full Tilt** (see entry).

Once we have overcome a personal disaster, illness or perhaps even turned a struggling business venture into a successful one, we may, with some relief, announce that we have now **Turned the Corner**. This is a naval expression and there are two corners to be turned, both of them at sea. The first is at the Cape of Good Hope on the southern tip of Africa and the second at Cape Horn, the most southerly part of South America. At both 'horns' two oceans collide and the sea is notoriously rough and dangerous for sailors. However, once each corner had been 'turned', going in either direction, the crew of a vessel could look forward to sailing in calmer waters for the rest of the voyage and put the horns behind them.

If you do not like the **Cut of Someone's Jib** then you generally dislike the way they look or what you hear about them. This phrase has its roots at sea and was in common use by 1823. In naval terms, the condition of something was known as the 'cut', while the 'jib' is the foresail that is responsible for the general performance of a ship. Hence the 'cut of its jib' refers to the overall condition of a sailing ship.

As the Crow Flies is a term we regularly use when defining the shortest distance between two points. When the tall ships first left England in search of the New World, without any maps, they always made sure they had cages full of crows on board. A crow, the navy believed, would always fly straight for the nearest point of land, once it had been released from the top of a mast. (That is why there is a 'crow's nest' up there.) The captain would then alter the ship's course in the direction of the crow's flight. This practice continued right up until the introduction of radar in the 1940s. Crows were particularly useful in British coastal waters during either foggy or stormy weather in helping a crew to find the nearest point of land.

A **Slush Fund** is a sum of money usually collected with little effort, or money from an investment or funding scheme that has not been designated for any other. It will then be spent in a co-operative way for the benefit of many. These days it is often used as a political term on both sides of the Atlantic. The original slush fund was found in galley kitchens beneath decks on the tall ships of the 17th and 18th centuries. In those pre-refrigerated days, meat would be preserved for many months by being salted and stored in large wooden barrels. Towards the end of a voyage, the empty barrels would be boiled and scraped, hence **Scraping the Barrel** (a phrase we use to describe accepting any circumstances available to us after we have run out of more favourable options). All the salt, including the fat drawn from the meat, would produce a 'slush', which was then sold ashore by the purser. The money raised would be collected into a fund, which was then used to buy luxuries for the whole crew (such luxuries as there were in those days). This practice was later extended to damaged cargo and war equipment, and the term 'slush fund' was firmly established by 1839. As usual it didn't take long for the politicians to hijack a naval phrase, and 'slush fund' soon came to mean a (possibly) illegal fund of money that has been established to pay people off with.

Going into even more detail, the word 'slush' derives from the Swedish word *slask*, meaning 'wet' and 'filthy'. The Old French word for 'cargo' is *arrumage*; hence the selling-off of anything damaged, unwanted or left over from a voyage quickly became known as a **Rummage Sale.**

*

Somebody who is **Aloof** is regarded as unapproach-able and keeps others at an emotional distance. This expression originates in the mid 16th century and comes from the Dutch word *loef*, meaning 'wind-ward'. Throughout the navy, a 'luff' then became the word meaning 'away and to windward', which would indicate a ship was sailing along a lee shore, setting her bows close to the wind and away from land, to prevent herself being blown ashore. From the land this would look as if a ship had her back to you, metaphorically speaking, with her head held high. Technically speaking, the ship was 'a luff' (aloof).

To be **On the Right Track** indicates a person is fol-lowing the correct procedure and is well on the way to resolving a problem successfully. This is actually a corruption of 'to be on the right tack', a nautical term. A sailing ship, heading into the wind, must plot a left-to-right, zig-zag type of path if it is to make any progress. This type of course is known as 'tacking', and to 'go off on the wrong tack' will lead to a ship making very little progress, or possibly none at all.

Dead Wood is the derogatory term given to that part of a working group or team that is not up to the standards of the others. The original 'dead wood' in a ship is the timber secured in the keel, which has no purpose at all other than to add weight and strength. This is also possibly where the expression **Dead Weight** comes from.

To **Knock Seven Bells** out of somebody is to hand out a serious beating, but not to actually knock the person unconscious. Of nautical origin and in regular use since around 1830, the expression is thought to have stemmed from the eight bells on board a ship. Hence to put only seven of them out of action meant to stop shy of making a complete job of it. The silencing of the ship's bells usually happened during times of war when opponents had rendered a vessel virtually ineffective.

A **Land Lubber** is a phrase used by sailors to describe a person who is much happier on dry land than they are at sea. In use since 1579, the expression is not a corruption of 'land lover', as many people believe. Instead, the source of the phrase can be traced to the word 'lubber', which was ship's language for a big, lumbering, clumsy novice. Adding the word 'land' only served to accentuate the insult coming from experienced seamen to a new sailor.

To be **Sent Up the Pole** means that you are being driven mad by something. The actual pole in question is a ship's mast, in particular the part above the rigging. On the high seas there was no more dangerous place to be, and one clearly must have taken leave of one's senses to climb up the pole, either willingly or otherwise (even experienced sailors didn't like going up there, which is why the ones who did received extra rum rations and pay), as a single mistake, or a single tot of rum too many, was likely to have disastrous consequences.

To stick by somebody **Through Thick and Thin**, or as some people say, 'like Posh and Becks', is to stand by a person or a venture and to remain loyal through the good times and the bad. This was originally a nautical expression and refers to the system of thick and thin pulleys enabling ropes of varying width to be used for hoisting the sails up and down.

You Scratch My Back and I'll Scratch Yours is a saying with its origins in the English navy. These days we use it to suggest two people will do each other a favour, or look out for each other, so that both parties may benefit from one another's actions. During the 17th and 18th centuries, the navy's punishments for disobedience or absenteeism were unimaginably harsh. It was common for a crew member to be tied to a mast after being sentenced to a dozen lashes with a 'cat o' nine tails', for very minor offences such as being drunk. A 'cat' was nine lengths of thin-knotted rope bound at one end into a handle. The flogging was usually carried out by one of the victim's shipmates in full view of the rest of the crew. But it was also likely that the shipmate would himself be a victim of the cat o' nine tails at some stage on a voyage, so would be lenient with his victim by applying only light strokes and merely 'scratching' the fellow's back. He himself would then receive equally lenient treatment by another shipmate if he was ever on the receiving end.

To finish the nautical section, I thought it might be a good idea to have a quick look at the **Captain's Log** (who's that sniggering at the back of class?), which is an instrument for measuring the speed of a ship through water (sometimes known as the 'maritime log'). The same name is also given to the daily record of events on board a ship, and in the case of an aircraft or a motor vehicle it is known as a 'logbook'. In the early years of sailing, prior to the introduction of modern instruments and accurate timepieces, officers used to literally drop a 'chip log' – a quarter-circle, flat piece of wood – into the sea from the bow of the ship. This was attached to a rope with knots tied into it at measured distances apart. At the aft of the vessel, a crewman would be waiting with a sandglass, also known as a 'log glass' and in modern times an 'hour glass'. As the knots passed by, the distances and times were recorded and a rough calculation of the speed could be made. This information was then noted down on the log itself. Also, quite obviously, this is where the term **Knot** comes from, meaning one nautical mile per hour. No wonder it took them so long to get anywhere in those days.

COUNTRY WISDOM

Touch Wood. If we are hoping for something to happen, or perhaps not to happen, the worst thing we can do is talk about it, because that is challenging fate to give us the outcome we are hoping for, which is never a good idea. The traditional way to ensure a favourable outcome once we have mentioned it is to find a nearby piece of wood and touch it. For centuries, people have touched wood in the hope of ensuring good fortune, and it is now such a natural response we do not even know that we are doing it, let alone why. Sir Winston Churchill once said that he always made sure he was within reaching distance of a piece of wood wherever he went.

Many authorities believe the tradition is Christian in origin and that the wood in question is that of a crucifix or a rosary. Others think it stems from the children's game of tag, and a participant is only safe when touching wood. There was also a children's game known as 'touch-iron', so there may be some truth in the theory, but I'm not convinced. A more plausible source for the term stems from the ancient beliefs of the Druids, who inhabited England before the Romans. They firmly believed that all the good and protective spirits in the world lived inside trees. People in distress or in need of good fortune would make their way to the designated tree to touch and hug it in the hope of finding peace and/or prosperity.

It Takes All Sorts is a phrase commonly used throughout the British Isles, frequently used to describe a person's unusual behaviour. On the one hand it can appear quite dismissive, while, on the other, it can be applied in a way that is more sympathetic and forgiving: 'I wouldn't worry much about Derek wearing ladies' clothing, if I were you: it takes all sorts to make up a world, you know.' The expression can also be slightly adjusted and used to imply surprising behaviour, without actually revealing what it is: 'You know that Derek; he gets up to all sorts, he does.' The phrase actually began life as a proverb and has been in use in England since the late 17th century, probably originating in the North. It was popularized nationally over two hundred years later by a new range of confectionery that came in all shapes, colours and flavours, and hence was called Liquorice All Sorts. Since these were launched in 1899, over two-thirds of the British population have eaten them at some time or other.

Our own **Kith and Kin** are people just like ourselves, either close relatives or respected, loyal and long-term friends. Originally, the word 'kith' meant neighbours or friends while 'kin' indicated 'blood relatives'. It was in the 1920s that the expression became regularly used when John Galsworthy published his book *In Chancery* (1920), which included the line: 'Its depleted bins preserved the record of family festivity: all the marriages, births and deaths of his kith and kin.' However, today we usually regard only close relatives as 'kith and kin'. For the sake of accuracy and detail, the Old English word for 'kith' was *cythth*, meaning 'relationship', and the word used for 'kin' was *cynn*, which meant 'family'.

*

The expression **As Dull as Dishwater** has changed slightly since the Middle Ages, when it was first used to describe anything, or indeed any person, that was not clear, bright and interesting, like a fast-running stream or a babbling brook. Instead, the object/person seemed boring and as dull as a ditch full of stagnant water and mud. 'As dull as ditchwater' was the phrase used at the time and it is easy to see how that has changed over the years, the comparison being made instead with dull and dirty *dishwater* after the washing-up has been done.

If someone has a **Gammy Leg** then one of their pins is not sufficiently strong to carry their full weight – it is a lame leg. But the term we should be using, in fact, is 'game leg'. 'Game' derives from the Irish word *cam*, meaning 'crooked'. It has been in use for centuries, right up until the 1950s, when 'game' started being pronounced 'gammy', so resulting in our modern expression. An example of how regularly it was once used in its original form can be found in George Orwell's *Down and Out in Paris and London* (1933): 'The room was an attic ten feet square, lighted only by a skylight, its sole furniture a narrow bedstead, a chair and a wash handstand with one game leg.'

To travel on **Shanks's Pony** means to have no transport at all – hence you will be making your way on foot. A variation of this was 'to go on Shanks's mare', which meant the same thing. The 'shank' is the part of the leg below the knee and above the ankle. Every one of us has a 'Shanks's pony' (i.e. the legs to transport us in place of a pony/horse).

We all know what a **Bare-faced Lie** is, don't we? It is an obvious lie told without any shame or guilt. In its original form, this expression indicated a fresh honesty, as a clean-shaven face could not conceal any untruths or hidden meanings, whereas all manner of slyness and duplicity could be hidden beneath a beard. In time, the phrase came to describe a person who didn't care whether or not they were lying and had no real intention of concealing their deception.

To **Blot Your Copybook** is to make a mistake, but not a particularly serious one. It means you are out of favour for a while until you can make amends. The expression originates from the time children used to learn to write using the newly introduced fountain pens and inkwells. Schools would provide children with two writing books, one for rough work, which could be full of crossed-out mistakes, misspellings and ink blots, and a copybook, which would be used for the finished work and presented to the teacher for appraisal. Children would be punished, although not severely, for 'blotting their copybooks' with ink stains.

Adding 'To Boot' to a sentence gives emphasis, suggesting we are gaining more than we originally
expected from an arrangement. Boots have nothing
to do with this Old English expression and instead
we should actually be using the word *bot*, which
can be translated as 'to gain advantage' or 'to profit'.
It is one of those many old words that have
come down through the ages, if in slightly altered
form.

The phrase to **Grasp the Nettle** means to face a
difficult situation positively and with confidence.
Stinging nettles are painful when brushed against
and can bring a person out in a nasty rash, but for
centuries they have been known for their healing
and nutritional value. Nettle soup, I am assured,
is a delicacy served now in the finest restaurants. I
am also assured that although nettles are painful
when touched lightly, if grabbed boldly they inflict
no pain or stinging sensation at all. Aaron Hill,
in his poem 'The Nettle's Lesson' (1743), endorses
this:

> *Tender-handed stroke a nettle,*
> *And it stings you for your pains,*
> *Grasp it like a man of mettle,*
> *And it soft as silk remains.*

There you are, kids – go off and try it. And tell your
mum Aaron Hill says it's OK.

Something in **Fine Fettle** is in good condition and ready for anything. In Old English, the word *fetel* originally meant 'strip of metal, girdle or binding' ('binding' is used here in the sense of getting things ready). However, over the years that shifted slightly to 'prepared, ready and in good condition', hence 'fine fettle'.

That's a **Whole New Kettle of Fish** is one of our more unusual idioms and one of the most difficult to explain, although its meaning is straightforward – 'another matter altogether' or a 'different situation'. Some research has suggested that the word 'kettle' in this case is a corruption of the Old English *kiddle*, which was a grille set across a river to catch passing fish. A fisherman might return to find poachers had helped themselves to the catch and left only weed and debris in the 'kettle'. Consequently, he might well claim that this was a 'different kettle of fish' to the one he was hoping for. However, a more likely origin can be found in the Scottish Border country where it was common for families and friends to spend the day feasting and socializing on the banks of a river. The main food of the day would be salmon, freshly caught in the river and cooked on a 'kettle' or barbecue. For this reason, the outings were known across Scotland as a 'kettle of fish' and there were many reasons or circumstances that could make one kettle of fish (day out) very different from another. One of the earliest recorded references can be found in Sir Walter Scott's book *St Ronan's Well* (1823), which includes the line: 'As the whole company go to the waterside today to eat a kettle of fish, there will be no risk of interruption.'

Lightning Never Strikes Twice is a phrase intended to offer consolation to someone after a recent misfortune, to remind them it is unlikely ever to happen again. It is an expression based on superstition, and one that might encourage us to tempt fate by doing something again in the belief that the same bad luck cannot repeat itself. But I have been in touch with NASA (the National Aeronautics and Space Administration, in America) and can confirm that lightning *does* strike in the same place more than once. NASA conducted a survey in Tucson, Arizona, during the summer of 1997 and found that within their sample of 386 flashes, 136 flashes (35 per cent) struck the ground in two or more places that were separated by mere tens of metres or less. There were a total of 558 different strike points; therefore, on average, each cloud-to-ground flash hit the earth in 1.45 places. So if you don't want to be hit by lightning then do not stand around in or near any place it has struck before, as it could happen again. That, and, obviously, don't move to Arizona.

To **Nip Something in the Bud** is to deal with a problem in the early stages in order to prevent an escalation. All of those who don their wellingtons of a weekend afternoon in spring will confirm they are not worried about snipping brand new shoots or buds from a developing plant as this pruning encourages stronger growth of the main stems and will result in healthier flowers and fruit in the long run. However, the use of the idiom has changed slightly over the years to suggest stopping 'unhealthy' growth rather than encouraging healthy development. The expression has been around for five hundred years or so, and if it had been made clearer from the outset, hundreds of schoolboys would not have been in trouble for pruning a prized plant at around an inch from the ground when asked merely to nip it in the bud.

Someone Just Walked Over My Grave is a remark often used when a person gets the shivers. This expression came about thanks to an old wives' tale, which is a legend, fable or story that is invariably both ridiculous and amazing and only ever believed by the naïve or gullible. The 'wives' in this instance believed that an involuntary shiver is felt when the place where a person will eventually be buried is being walked upon, and this was seen as a reminder of that person's mortality. The phrase an **Old Wives' Tale** was made popular in 1595 when George Peel produced a play of the same name, featuring wicked witches and fanciful and outrageous events masquerading as factual. Mind you, there are some modern ex-wives' tales I could tell that would make your hair curl in disbelief.

To **Sow Your Wild Oats** is a phrase applied to the pursuit of wild, possibly illegal and undoubtedly immoral practices while in the full bloom of youth. The expression has been in use for over four centuries, deriving from the notion that impulsive young men would scatter only wild and uncultured seed here, there and everywhere, while older men, being wiser and more experienced, would take care to sow their cultivated seed only on fertile ground. Wild oats (or wild seed) produce weeds that are hard to get rid of and consequently cause many problems, but a man of experience has learned how to avoid all of that. The expression passed over to wider use in 1829 with a line from William Cobbett: 'The vices of youth are varnished over by the saying that there must be a time for the sowing of wild oats.' From this arose the loosely connected term **Getting Your Oats**, referring to indulgence in regular sexual activity for either sex. But when we consider the actual meaning of the expression – 'to be getting your share of seed' – it rather loses its youthful, romantic sense, especially when applied to the fairer sex. Personally, I think it is high time young people were banned from enjoying themselves and that the sowing of wild oats was left to the more mature, who really know how to have fun.

*

To **Put a Spoke in Someone's Wheel** means to deliberately disrupt their plans and restrict progress. This phrase has often caused confusion, especially as most wheels these days already have spokes, so that an extra spoke may not seem much of a hindrance at all – quite sporty-looking, in fact. In the Middle Ages, however, horse-drawn carts all had wheels made out of solid, circular, wooden discs. Holes were bored through the front wheels into which a pole or a peg, known as the 'spoke', could be placed, like a form of brake, in order to either restrict the speed of the wheel (when going downhill) or stop the cart altogether. The word 'spoke' was first recorded in the early 1600s and derives from the Dutch word *speek*, which became *spike* in Old English and later developed into the word 'spoke'.

To be **Working Up to the Collar** implies putting in real effort to get a job done. The 'collar' referred to here is one worn by a horse or ox when pulling a heavy cart or perhaps a plough. Animals who worked with the collar straining tightly around their shoulders were obviously pulling heavy loads and therefore working extremely hard, while those with the collar set more loosely around their necks were clearly not having to drag such heavy weights and therefore not working to their full capacity. It is a farming expression that has been part of the English language for centuries.

*

To **Have a Hunch** about something is to have an instinctive feeling about an outcome. This expression is American in origin, dating from the early 1900s. It derives from a gambling superstition that suggested rubbing the hump of a hunchback would bring good fortune. This in turn stems from a medieval belief that hunchbacks were possessed and empowered by the devil to see into the future.

By Hook or by Crook is an expression we use to describe achieving something by any means possible, whether honest or not. There are two suggested origins for this expression and for the first we need to understand that the 'hook' in question is a blunt bill-hook and the 'crook' the hooked staff a shepherd used to gather his flock. In feudal England during the Middle Ages, a law was passed preventing the cutting down of trees or lopping of branches to make firewood. But the law permitted the poor to gather dead wood from forests and deemed anything they could collect with a blunt hook or shepherd's crook was allowable. The *Bodmin Register* (1525) states: 'Dynmure Wood is open to the inhabitants of Bodmin . . . to bear away on their backs a burden of lop, hook, crook and bag wood.'

The second suggested source for the expression

takes us to Ireland, which during the 17th century had become the centre of Royalist activity and a potential base of operations for Charles Stuart, the son of Charles I, after the Parliamentarians came to power. In 1649, the New Model Army planned an invasion, but Cromwell had been warned that Waterford City, in southern Ireland, was impossible to invade by sea as that would have meant sailing along the River Suir, which left the fleet vulnerable to attack. Instead, Cromwell (see **Warts and All**) announced he would invade on the Wexford side of the city, from Hook Head, and from the west side at a place called Crook. 'I will conquer Ireland by the Hook or by the Crook,' he announced. Both locations still appear on any detailed map of Ireland and the lighthouse at Hook Head claims to be the oldest in the British Isles.

GOING TO WAR

The **Backroom Boys** are a group of people, male or female, who work away quietly, developing new ideas that would be of particular benefit to industry or commerce. For example, scientists who are hard at work developing new products for a particular company might be nicknamed 'backroom boys'. In offices, administrators keep the whole business running smoothly with little or no thanks for their efforts, and they would also be known as backroom boys. The phrase was coined during the Second World War when Lord Beaverbrook, who was minister of aircraft production at the time, made a radio broadcast on 19 March 1941 during which he credited his research department for some inspiring inventions that helped to change the direction of the war: 'Let me say that the credit belongs to the boys in the backroom. It isn't the man who sits in the limelight who should have the praise. It is not the men who sit in prominent places. It is the boys in the backrooms who do.' But the phrase can actually be traced back to America in the 1870s, so possibly Beaverbrook had heard it before, although there is no doubt it was he who brought it into regular use in England.

To **Hit the Ground Running** is a phrase used on both sides of the Atlantic to describe a person or event getting off to a successful start, straight into action. Originally it was an American phrase, which can be traced directly to the military training schools of both the First and Second World Wars. Foot soldiers, paratroopers and marines were all trained extensively to jump and land on their feet, either from boats, aircraft or jeeps, so they could get on with the business at hand without delay. 'Hit the ground running' was a frequently heard shout from the training officer on manoeuvres and the expression had become widespread by the end of the Second World War. It had passed into regular usage by the time of the business boom during the 1980s when rapid success was a defining feature of the decade. A closely associated expression is probably even more widely used, and it is easy to see how those who stumbled when they did not quite hit the ground running might soon be **Up and Running** after a slow start.

*

Umpteen is not exactly a phrase or even idiom, but still well worth recording. It is a word we use to describe a randomly large amount. With my mum it was always: 'I have told you umpteen times not to do that.' During the First World War, army signallers used Morse code, which is a sequence of dots and dashes, to send and receive vital messages, and this was an invaluable method of communication. For reasons that are not clear, the word 'umpty' became slang for a single dash and by borrowing the 'teen' part of sixteen, seventeen, eighteen, etc., the word for a large number of dashes in a sequence became 'umpteen'.

To have **Bought the Farm** is a well-known American expression meaning 'to have died'. There are several suggested origins, one being a sentimental line in a US war film, which has a character from the Mid West yearning for home and telling friends that when the war is over he plans to return to the country, buy a farm and settle down. When the character is later killed in action, his buddy sentimentally remarks: 'Well, I guess Joe has bought his farm now.' The popularity of the film at the time ensured the phrase passed over into wider use in the States, especially during the Korean War, when it was suggested fallen comrades had 'bought the farm'. The second suggested, and more likely, origin leads us to the early days of aviation when the great pioneers were invariably rich playboys, such as **Gordon Bennett** (see entry), who were living life on the edge of danger. If and when aircraft crashed into farms or remote farmland, the estate of the deceased pilot would be held responsible for any damage and was invariably forced to pay substantial costs. Such payments would usually be enough for the farmer to redeem a mortgage or to buy a farm outright. Dead aviators were thus often known to have paid for or 'bought the farm'.

There is another possibility, however. During the Second World War, US servicemen were all given life insurance policies worth US$10,000 – a great deal of money in the 1940s. Most young and unmarried servicemen named their parents as beneficiaries and those killed in action could be known to have 'bought the farm'. The expression, often shortened to **Bought It**, is not used as frequently in England, where the alternatives are **Kicked the Bucket** and **Gone for a Burton** (see entries).

Finally, some believe the phrase has a religious origin, on the basis that the Old Testament refers to heaven as 'a farm for the soul'. A person killed, especially in the service of the good Lord, had a place in heaven, hence 'bought the farm'. Like I say, some believe it, but I'm not one of them.

Gone for a Burton is a phrase used to indicate somebody has had an unfortunate mishap, or that something or someone has been lost altogether. Before the Second World War, Burton's Ales ran an advert depicting a football team with one player missing from the line-up, leaving a gap in the team photograph. The caption explained that the player had 'gone for a Burton'. This slogan was picked up by the RAF during the war and used as slang for a missing pilot who invariably had crashed in action into the sea (or 'the drink') and was affectionately referred to as having 'gone for a Burton'. He would be missing from the photographs in future.

To **Camp It Up** is to perform in an effeminate and flamboyant manner in an attempt to draw attention to oneself. Quite how this phrase became applied to overt homosexuality isn't known, but it is recorded that trails or groups of civilians would follow a marching army, providing various services such as sales of alcohol, washer women or male and female prostitutes. As they would also camp nearby, this could perhaps be where the associated expression **Camp as a Row of Tents** derives from.

To have **More Than You Can Shake a Stick At** is to have far more of anything than you really need. This expression is said to have a farming origin, in particular sheep farming. If a shepherd had more sheep than he could control with his crook (stick) then it is easy to see how the term came to be applied. However, another school of thought suggests an American origin of a military kind. After George Washington was once seen waving a ceremonial wooden sword over the British troops he had recently defeated, other American generals began to use the expression to justify themselves when they had not been quite as successful as the great man himself was in battle. 'We had more men to fight than you could wave a stick at' was apparently a common excuse for failure on the battlefield.

If someone has had their **Guns Spiked** it suggests they have had their plans foiled. The earliest type of battlefield cannon was muzzle loaded and the only way it could be fired was by igniting gunpowder through a small charge-hole. In a simple but effective piece of military disruption, an enemy could put a gun out of action for a long time, sometimes even permanently, by driving a small metal spike deep into the charge-hole, which would seal it completely. It was a tricky job for a blacksmith to remove it and consequently just a handful of undercover agents could neutralize many of an army's guns in a very short time by using this method of sabotage. It was also possible to 'spike' one of two duelling weapons thereby ensuring a favourable outcome for a so-called gentleman. These days you are more likely to find it is your drink that is 'spiked', although in a different way and for different reasons.

A **Turncoat** is someone who is happy to side with one group of people and show loyalty, but will soon switch sides if it suits their purpose and without a moment's remorse or hesitation, either. The term 'turncoat' seems, on the face of it, a difficult one to work out, although it is sometimes thought the expression refers to retreating soldiers who turned their coats around and wore them back to front in the hope nobody would realize they were actually running away rather than still facing the enemy. But this explanation seems little better than ridiculous to me. Let's face it: if this were true then the retreating soldier would also have to reverse his hat, trousers and shoes, shave the back of his head, paint a face and moustache on, and then perform a sort of reverse shuffle for this to look even nearly genuine. But if he did try that, then he would certainly be safe, as his enemy would be laughing too hard to shoot straight anyway. It can't be true.

Instead, there is a wonderful story behind the phrase that I find much more plausible. During the Hundred Years War in the 14th and 15th centuries, the Duke of Saxony – whose land occupied an area long fought over by the French and the English – cleverly had a coat made for himself (or so legend has it) which was blue on one side and white on the other. When the French army was on his land, he made sure he wore it white side outwards (the French colour) in an effort to show his allegiance, and yet when the English army gained ground, he immediately turned it around and wore it as a blue coat, affecting loyalty to them. The expression became widely known through Shakespeare's play *The Taming of the Shrew* (1597), which refers to the practice of 'turning one's garments around' in tune with the opinion of others. (See also **Double Cross**.)

To **Use Your Loaf** means to show common sense and intelligence. I would love to find an interesting origin for this, but in fact it derives from the simple 'use your loaf of bread', meaning 'head' in cockney rhyming slang. There is a second suggestion for the origin of this phrase, one that can be found in the archives of the American Civil War. The story tells us that Confederate soldiers would receive a freshly baked loaf of bread each day as part of their ration. When engaging Federal positions, soldiers were known to spear their loaf with a bayonet, place a hat upon it and hold it up from their covered position to see if the bobbing 'head' attracted any gunfire. This practice was apparently known as 'using your loaf'. I can't find any solid evidence for it, but it is a good story even so.

When somebody is described as a **Loose Cannon**, they can be regarded as unreliable, unpredictable and dangerous. The expression is said to be American in origin and related to US artillerymen who fired their cannons during the Civil War both randomly and inaccurately, sometimes even at their own men. 'Friendly fire' they call it these days. However, others believe this to be an English nautical term, as during sea battles a heavy cannon breaking loose from its berth would slide all over the gun deck, killing or injuring any sailor in its path. Hence the cry would go up: 'Beware the loose cannon!'

No Quarter Asked For and No Quarter Given means that no leniency is expected or will be given under any circumstances, usually in the business arena or on the sports field. Originally the expression was used on the battlefield and, rather ominously, the word 'quarter' is the old English word for 'mercy'. A defeated army could possibly cry out for 'quarter' while surrendering, but usually pride and foolish bravery prevented them from doing so. Instead, they would accept any punishment meted out by their enemy. The expression can often be found in historic military records in reference to captured prisoners.

The expression **AWOL** is something we might apply to a friend or colleague whose absence cannot be explained as they are not wherever they should be. Originally, in military terms at least, the expression meant 'missing without permission' and was applied to soldiers who were absent for a short period of time and then returned to their ranks. During the American Civil War, offenders were forced to wear a placard around their necks with the initials AWOL printed on it, which stood for 'Absent With Out Leave'. As they were not strictly deserters, the only punishment they had to endure was public shame. During the First World War, the expression was still being pronounced as individual letters, and it was only as the Second World War drew to a close that 'AWOL' started to be said as an acronym. Contrary to popular belief, the expression does not mean 'absent without *official* leave'.

A **Diehard Supporter** is resilient, fierce and will show complete loyalty in any circumstances. The original group of 'diehards' were the British 57th Foot Regiment, in the Duke of Wellington's army, who fought bravely against the French during the Battle of Albuhera. On 16 May 1811, their commanding officer, Colonel Inglis, had his horse shot dead from beneath him and he himself lay badly injured on the ridge that was a key position for Wellington's army. At that time, the English were outnumbered by French troops and under heavy attack. But even so, Inglis refused all attempts to carry him to the rear and instead lay shouting encouragement to his men: 'Die Hard the 57th, Die Hard.' I am not sure if that sort of motivational speaking would encourage me much, but it worked at the time and the battle was eventually won – albeit with heavy casualties as only one of the 24 officers survived, along with 168 out of the original 584 infantrymen.

From that day onwards, the regiment, which became the 'West Middlesex Regiment', were known throughout Wellington's army as the 'diehards'. It is not recorded what the French army called the diehards after the event, but we can have fun guessing.

The original **Dumdum Bullet** was developed by the British military and, based on the jacketed .303 bullets, had its nose open to expose the lead core. This meant that on impact the soft-nosed shells would rip open and cause massive internal damage to its intended (human) target. Originally designed at the Dum Dum Arsenal and used on the northwest frontier of India in the late 1890s, they were soon outlawed by The Hague Convention of 1889. However, the United States refused to ratify the convention and so it never became international law in any war involving the US army, which, let's face it, is most of them in one way or another. The reason they refused to agree was that American troops were busy at the time using expanding bullets on the Filipinos, whom they had recently liberated from Spanish rule. A special note published with the convention explained the reasoning at the time:

NOTE: Dumdum bullets, first manufactured by the British at Dum Dum, India, are of advantage only in jungle warfare against primitive tribes, where the danger is of sudden rushes of large numbers at close quarters. They are not used in European warfare because they are inaccurate and tend to foul guns. If they offered an advantage, they would be used regardless of any treaty.

The expression 'dumdum' has since been affectionately applied to any other soft-nosed cartridge designed to leave its victim's insides hanging in tatters.

Anybody who is **Gung Ho** is bullish, aggressive and highly enthusiastic, usually failing to take many important factors into account before taking decisive action. This expression was originally applied to Carlson's Raiders, who were a moderately successful marine guerrilla unit operating in the South Pacific during the Second World War between 1942 and 1946. Their commanding officer, Evans F. Carlson, spent many years in China prior to the war, developing his battle strategies by observing Chinese teamwork and comradeship. In China the term *kung ho* means 'working closely together' and this is where Carlson found his phrase. But the term became differently construed as a result of Carlson's bullish and sometimes irresponsible attitude, which famously included, at one time, leaving nine of his men stranded on Makin Island, who were later captured and beheaded by the Japanese.

To **Get Your Kit Off** means to undress completely. This is of recent origin and applied to removing military kit, although in the early 1990s British journalists began to apply it to actresses, actors and anyone else stripping naked. An article in the *Daily Telegraph* on 29 April 1994 sowed the seed when it reported: 'In the late Sixties and early Seventies directors banged on endlessly about the artistic integrity of their nude scenes, though it was strange, as Bernard Levin perceptively observed, that only pretty women seemed to be required to get their kit off. Chaps still clung cravenly to their Y-Fronts and older, uglier women were generally spared strip-tease duties.'

Go Tell It to the Marines is a well-known expression, especially in America, that is used in response to an unbelievable story or suggestion. The phrase originated in England when the marines were considered inferior to regular soldiers and sailors as they worked on both land and sea and so were regarded by many as expert at neither, therefore stupid. The idiom, which was in regular use at the time of the Battle of Trafalgar in 1805, was originally 'tell that to the marines because the sailors won't believe it'. It was in this full form that John Moore used it in *The Post Captain* (1810) and just over a decade later, in *The Island* (1823), Byron is suggesting it is an old saying by putting it into an historical setting:

'. . . But whatsoe'er betide, ah, Neuha! Now
Unman me not; the hour will not allow
A tear; I'm thine, whatever intervenes!'
'Right,' quoth Ben; 'that will do for the marines.'

I'd challenge anyone to make sense of that – now or then. The expression became popular again (in a rather more comprehensible form this time) thanks to a story told by Major W. P. Drury in *The Tadpole of an Archangel* (1904). Drury later admitted his story was a pure invention and a 'leg-pull of my youth', but it is still how the phrase passed into wider use. In his book, Drury describes an entry in Samuel Pepys's *Diary*, from 1664, in which Pepys attended a banquet given by Charles II who was entertaining guests with a far-fetched naval tale about flying fish. The story had everybody laughing in disbelief, except for an officer in the marines who insisted he had seen such fish for himself. The king was convinced and announced that if the marines, with their vast experience of the high seas, had seen such a thing, then the story must be true. He also announced that if he heard such fanciful tales again, he would check the truth of them by first telling the marines. Drury's story had historians frantically checking Pepys's *Diary* and after an exhaustive search it was revealed there was no such entry. It was only then that Drury admitted he had made it up completely. No doubt he had spent the intervening time laughing at all the attention surrounding his book – all the way to the bank too, I would imagine.

Iron Rations is a term we use for 'emergency supplies', usually to be carried about the person. Originally the phrase indicated military rations made up principally of tinned food, but more recently it has been applied to any basic food that is easy to prepare and consume, carried by mountaineers, cyclists and other travellers or sportsmen and women.

When someone is described as **Shell Shocked**, they are stunned and momentarily debilitated by something they have seen or heard. During the First World War, soldiers experienced the introduction of heavy artillery and explosives such as had never been seen before in the field of conflict. It was during the trench warfare of 1915, after almost constant shelling from enemy guns, that a significant number of Allied casualties, suffering from what was described as shell shock, were reported. This was a relatively unheard-of disorder – although first reported during the Russian–Japanese War of 1904–5 – that resulted in young men suffering from a wide range of both physical and psychological problems. Previously, such symptoms had been dismissed as either cowardice or malingering and were usually 'treated' with severe punishment. The First World War proved to be a turning point in attitudes towards sufferers, as this statement by company quarter-master Sergeant Gordon Fisher, found in the military archives, illustrates:

I went further along and looked into the next dug-out and there was a guardsman in there. They talk about the psychology of fear. He was a perfect example. I can see that guardsman now! His face was yellow, he was shaking all over, and I said to him, 'What the hell are you doing here?' He said, 'I can't go. I can't do it. I daren't go!' Now, I was pretty ruthless in those days and I said to him, 'Look, I'm going up the line and when I come back if you're still here I'll bloody well shoot you!' . . . when I came back, thank God, he'd gone. He was a Coldstream. A big chap six foot tall. He'd got genuine shell shock. We didn't realize that at the time. We used to think it was cowardice, but we learned later on that there was such a thing as shell shock. Poor chap, he couldn't help it. It could happen to anybody.

The symptoms soldiers faced after heavy shelling were in the form of amnesia, insomnia, severe anxiety, depression, alcoholism, irritability and frightening flashbacks of the traumatic event. After the war, many victims continued to suffer and men were frequently reduced to a state of stunned immobility at the slightest surprise, which led to the term 'shell shock' being applied to a stunned and fearful reaction to events of any kind.

Bloody Sunday is the name best known in Britain as the day the Parachute Regiment clashed with demonstrators, during a banned civil rights protest, at Londonderry in Northern Ireland on Sunday 30 January 1972, killing 13 civilians in the process. However, Ireland's original Bloody Sunday is the name given to Sunday 21 November 1920, when members of Sinn Fein murdered 14 British undercover intelligence agents in cold blood. Prior to that, in Russia, Sunday 22 January 1905 was the day thousands of unarmed peasants, led peacefully by Father Gapon, attempted to hand in a petition to the tsar at the Winter Palace in St Petersburg. Hundreds were mown down at the gates when the Russian army opened fire, which was an incident also known as Bloody Sunday and sowed the seeds for the Russian Revolution, which culminated in the Red Army storming the same palace in 1917. But the *original* Bloody Sunday took place earlier than that. In 1887, the Chief Secretary for Ireland, Arthur Balfour (see **Bob's Your Uncle**), had ordered the arrest and prosecution of William O'Brien, the Irish Nationalist leader. O'Brien's supporters quickly arranged an assembly at Mitchelstown in County Cork, which was then broken up by the police, who fired upon the gathering. Three people were killed and many injured, earning Balfour the nickname

'Bloody Balfour' throughout Ireland. As a reaction to O'Brien's imprisonment and the horror of Mitchelstown, a socialist demonstration in protest of the events was arranged later that year in Trafalgar Square, London, on Sunday 13 November. However, Balfour's uncle, British prime minister Robert Gascoyne-Cecil (aka Lord Salisbury), declared the rally illegal and the subsequent police baton charge left two protesters beaten to death in the shadow of Nelson's Column in what was the first Bloody Sunday.

To **Steal a March** on a person is to gain an advantage by taking action before they either realize what is happening or are ready for it. This is a military expression and dates to around 1770, revealing the tactic of an army marching through the night, while their enemy slept, in order to occupy a strategic position, ready to fight, before the enemy had even woken up and thought what to have for breakfast.

THE WORLD OF BOOKS

A **Collins** is a letter of thanks to a person for their hospitality. Instead of a simple 'thank you', it will be an elaborate piece written to impress the recipient. These days it is not a very well-known term, probably because few of us have the time or manners to go to such trouble. But the word was widely used in the 1800s after the novelist Jane Austen had one of her characters, in *Pride and Prejudice* (1813), threatening to send such a letter to the Bennet family following a stay at their country house. The character in question was a sycophantic clergyman called Mr Collins.

To **Bell the Cat** is a wonderful expression used to describe any dangerous task carried out at great personal risk. The origin of this phrase and why we use it can be found in William Langland's *Piers Plowman*

(1377). This contains the tale of a family of mice who were constantly being terrorized by the fat, grumpy cat of the neighbourhood. One day the mouse household held a family meeting to discuss how they could best deal with the sur-prise attacks and the youngest mouse came up with the notion of tying a bell around the cat's neck, so that all the mice would be able to hear him coming. This idea delighted all the others and they danced around in celebration until the wisest old mouse said, 'That's all very well, but who will actually bell the cat?' (No one did in the end.)

There is a delightful example of this phrase in action in Scottish history. During the late 1480s, the nobility became deeply suspicious of King James III's apparently homosexual relationship with his favourite new architect, a man called Cochran. Members of court met in secret and discussed ways of eliminating Cochran, who had been affecting their own relationships with the king. As the meeting came to a close, the unanimous decision was that he should be killed, whereupon Lord Gray asked, 'Well, who will bell the cat then?' Archibald Douglas, the feisty Earl of Angus, immediately replied, 'I will bell this cat.' The earl went out at once and seized the unfor-tunate Cochran and hanged him under the bridge

THE WORLD OF BOOKS

at Lauder. It was an act that earned him the nickname 'Bell-the-cat Douglas'.

There have been periods throughout history when
the phrase was more in use than at other times. In
1880, James Payn wrote:

'Mrs and Miss Jennynge must bell the cat' [said Mrs
Armytage.]

'What have I to do with cats?' inquired Mrs Jennynge
wildly. 'I hate cats.'

'My dear madam, it is a well-known proverb,'
explained Mrs Armytage. 'What I mean is, that it is you
who should ask Mr Josceline to say grace this evening.'

Ten years later, Walter Scott wrote in his *Journal*
(1890): 'A fine manly fellow, who has belled the cat
with fortune.'

To **Write Like an Angel** means either to have stylish
and elegant handwriting, or to be a
gifted poet or writer of prose.
Which probably explains
why I have never had this
expression addressed to
me. It is a strange phrase,
and while it is easy to see
how a person may 'sing',
'fly' or even 'sound' like an
angel, how can we 'write' like
one?

The answer can be found way back

in the 16th century with a Greek writer called Angelo Vergetgo, whose amazing calligraphy impressed the great and the good of the entire European continent. Later, Francis I of France had a Greek fount cast that was modelled on Angelo's writing style. Later still, in the latter part of the 19th century, a scholar named Henry Stephens was regarded as one of the most elegant calligraphers of *his* time, and when it was discovered he had learned his craft from studying the writing of Angelo himself, his own name also became synonymous with beautiful writing. It was recorded that he 'wrote like Angelo', giving rise to the expression which has been in use for thousands of years and still holds today. David Garrick, the English actor and founder of the famous Garrick Club in London, wrote a humorous epitaph in 1775: 'Here lies poet Goldsmith, for shortness called Noll, who wrote like an angel, but talked like poor Poll.' As for me, I can't see what all the fuss is about.

To be **Grinning Like a Cheshire Cat** is to be very pleased with yourself and constantly smiling, perhaps somewhat foolishly. There are several possibilities for the root of this phrase, including the mysterious Cheshire Cat appearing and then disappearing in Lewis Carroll's *Alice's Adventures in Wonderland* (1865). In the story, the Cheshire Cat gradually fades away until only his grin remains. The book became so popular all over the world that many regard this as the source of the expression. However, the phrase, and the related one, **Cheesy Grin**, has long been in use and is thought to relate to the face of a grinning cat stamped on all cheeses produced in Cheshire since the 12th century, although it is claimed by some that the Romans introduced cheese making to the county a thousand years before even then.

We also know that high on the front wall of Birkenhead Priory, the Benedictine monastery established in 1150, a gargoyle in the shape of a grinning cat sits towards the end of the orig-inal entrance arch. And we know about the carved cat found on the front of the medieval building cov-ering the holy well of St Winefrid at Holywell, but neither of these is actually in Cheshire. A few cen-turies later, the historian Ewart tells the tale of one of Richard III's gamekeepers, apparently a monster of a man called Caterling who permanently wore a wide and evil-looking grin. Ewart suggests the phrase was originally 'to grin like a Cheshire Caterling' and later shortened. If this is true, then the phrase dates to the late 1400s, long before Lewis Carroll, but long after the cheese makers had adopted a smiling cat as their logo.

Finally we have Peter Pinder (nom de plume of John Walcot MD), who wrote in *A Pair of Lyric*

Epistles (1795): 'Lo! Like a Cheshire Cat our court will grin'. Either way, it appears that Lewis Carroll had been influenced by at least one of these stories (among other things – if his books are anything to go by), but there is little doubt that it is due to *Alice's Adventures in Wonderland* that the expression began to be used all over the world by the late 19th century and was no longer confined to Cheshire.

When we are going **Hell for Leather** we are going as fast as we possibly can, usually in a clumsy and uncontrolled manner. When riding as fast as this, a horseman was certainly putting a lot of wear into his leather saddle, thereby 'exchanging hell for leather'. Rudyard Kipling may well have coined the phrase in his book *The Story of Gadsbys* (1899).

A **Blue Stocking** is an expression used to describe a clever and intellectual woman, and there are two possible explanations for the term. First, in Venice in 1400, a secret society of high-minded men and women was formed calling themselves *della calza*, which means 'of the stocking'. They created a crest, which had blue stockings as its emblem, and the idea was copied in Paris in 1590 where members of the *Bas Bleu* (blue stocking) followed suit. This proved to be so popular with the ladies of intellect that in 1750 Lady Elizabeth Montague opened her own house to like-minded scholars and leading literary figures of the day, who would while away the time sharing ideas and fantasies with each other. With the emphasis of such discussion being on learning and the arts, the fashion sense sometimes left a little to be desired. One of the more prominent members of Lady Montague's group was Benjamin Stillingfleet, who preferred to wear blue silk stockings with his evening suit instead of the customary black worn by the other gentlemen of his era. With London society generally a little more cynical and unforgiving than their French or Italian counterparts, the group were frequently ridiculed and quickly nicknamed 'the blue stocking society', thanks to Stillingfleet's dress sense.

An **Albatross Around One's Neck** is considered to be a lifelong burden from which there is no escape. In 'The Rime of the Ancient Mariner' (from *Lyrical Ballads and a Few Other Poems*, 1798), Samuel Taylor Coleridge tells the story of a sailor whose ship was trapped by ice and who was visited by an albatross. The bird was regarded as a lucky symbol at sea and, sure enough, soon afterwards the vessel was freed from the ice. But then the hapless mariner shot the albatross and almost instantly a curse befell the ship. The furious crew hung the dead bird around the sailor's neck as a punishment, but one by one each of them died, eventually leaving the mariner alone. Then, while watching the beautiful seasnakes in the water around the ship, the mariner began blessing them and the albatross dropped from his neck. The ship was freed once again and the sailor's life had been saved. From then on, the man travelled the earth telling his tale and encouraging love for all God's creatures. The moral of the story is that an albatross is a symbol of personal guilt, and freedom from it must be earned.

Big Brother is a phrase we have come to use to describe being watched over by the authorities at all times. It is one of the most frequently employed idioms today, thanks to a certain popular reality television show. In 1948, George Orwell wrote his classic dystopian novel *Nineteen Eighty-four* in which the government exercises dictatorial control by watching the every move of its citizens. Orwell called this cynical, oppressive head of a totalitarian state Big Brother:

On each landing, opposite the lift-shaft, the poster gazed from the wall. It depicted simply an enormous face, more than a metre wide: the face of a man of about forty-five, with a heavy black moustache and ruggedly handsome features. It was one of those pictures which are so contrived that the eyes follow you about when you move. BIG BROTHER IS WATCHING YOU, the caption beneath it ran. Nobody has ever seen BIG BROTHER. He is a face on the hoardings, a voice on the telescreen. We may be reasonably sure he will never die, and there is already considerable uncertainty as to when he was born. BIG

BROTHER is infallible and all-powerful.

Also featured in the book is the dreaded **Room 101**, where you would be tortured by the thing you feared the most, and from which it was thought nobody would ever return. Incidentally, Room 101 was the office Orwell had assigned to him at the BBC when he worked for the corporation during the Second World War.

You may find yourself **In the Doghouse** if you are not careful, and that is no place to be, believe you me. The expression is traditionally applied to a husband, or male partner, who is unable to behave himself and is held in disgrace. The source of this expression is found in J. M. Barrie's *Peter Pan* (1904) and the character Mr Darling, who is made to live in the dog kennel by his wife as a result of his behaviour towards 'Nana'. He is only allowed to return to the house when his children return from Neverland.

Another idiom from popular literature is a **Dog in the Night-time** – a phrase we might use to describe an unsuspecting conniver, someone who has unwittingly involved themselves in a crime. Sir Arthur Conan Doyle invented the dog in question when he published the Sherlock Holmes adventure 'Silver Blaze' in 1892. In the story, the family dog would not bark during the night when horses were being stolen from the stable, because it knew the man who had taken them. The following exchange between Holmes and Inspector Gregory has since become world famous:

'Is there any point to which you would like to draw my attention?'
  'To the curious incident of the dog in the night time.'
  'The dog did nothing in the night time?'
  'That was the curious incident,' remarked Holmes.

Mark Haddon's *The Curious Incident of the Dog in the Night-time* (2002), in which the dog itself is the victim, clearly had the world-famous detective in mind as the teenage hero sets out to look for clues for the killing (his 'dogged' approach having unexpected consequences).

When we hear the phrase **Dropping Like Flies** we know we are losing people at a rapid pace. The expression derives from the popular children's fairy tale 'The Brave Little Tailor' by the Brothers Grimm. In the story the main character, a tailor, kills seven flies with a cloth and then makes himself a belt to celebrate the needless slaughter. The belt, which is decorated with the words *Seven at One Blow*, sets off a chain of misunderstandings and adventures that lead to the tailor becoming king of the land.

A **Goody Two Shoes** is a person who behaves in an impeccable manner but is perhaps sometimes a little smug about this. The expression is another of those lifted directly from literature and the imagination of a creative writer, in this case Irishman Oliver Goldsmith. In 1765, Goldsmith released his latest children's tale, entitled, in the characteristically long-winded style of the time, 'The History of Little Goody Two Shoes, otherwise called Mrs Margery Two Shoes, with the Means by Which She Acquired Her Learning and Wisdom, and in Consequence Thereof her Estate; Set Forth at Large for the Benefit of Those Who From a State of Rags and Care and Having Shoes but Half a Pair; Their Fortune and their Fame Would Fix, and Gallop in a Coach and Six'. (Despite this, it still sold in large numbers, apparently.) John Newbery then published Goldsmith's tale, in which the central character owned only one shoe, although when she was finally given a pair for being good, she proudly showed them off to everybody, exclaiming 'look, two shoes' – and hence the expression was created.

A **Hooray Henry** is a disparaging term used in Britain to describe a loud-mouthed, upper-class, public school idiot. Jim Godbolt coined the phrase in 1951 when he used it to describe the fans of Old Etonian jazz trumpeter Humphrey Lyttelton who would turn up in droves to the 100 Club in Oxford Street, London, to hear him play. Between songs, Lyttelton's supporters could be identified by the loud, upper-class voices shouting 'Hooray, Hooray'. The full expression derives from a character in Damon Runyon's story 'Tight Shoes' (1936) who is described as 'strictly a Hoorah Henry'. Lyttelton himself seemed to confirm this association, while distancing himself from the term, when he said, during an interview: 'In jazz circles, aggressively "upper-class" characters are known as Hoorays, an adaptation, I believe, of Damon Runyon's "Hooray Henries".'

The phrase **Two Ships that Pass in the Night** is used to describe people who encounter each other briefly, despite often being in the same place at roughly the same time on more than one occasion. The expression is lifted directly from popular literature and in particular a poem from Henry Wadsworth Longfellow's collection *Tales from a Wayside Inn* (1863):

Ships that pass in the night, and speak with each other in passing,
Only a signal shown and a distant voice in the darkness,
So on the ocean of life we pass and speak to one another,
Only a look and a voice and darkness again and silence.

Longfellow holds the distinction of being considered the first professional American poet. Many lines from his works have passed into the English language, the most famous of these being **The Patter of Tiny Feet**, which comes from his poem 'The Children's Hour' (1860), an ode to his three daughters Alice, Allegra and Edith:

Between the dark and the daylight,
When the night is beginning to lower,
Comes a pause in the day's occupations,
That is known as the Children's Hour.

I hear in the chamber above me
The patter of little feet,
The sound of a door that is opened
And voices soft and sweet.

To call somebody an **Uncle Tom** is a derogatory reference implying a black person has an unduly deferential and reverential attitude to white people. The expression derives from Harriet Beecher Stowe's novel *Uncle Tom's Cabin* (1852), which depicted a faithful and dignified old black man called Uncle Tom. Black activists and human rights campaigners later argued that the story, or 'Uncle Tomism' as it became known, was detrimental to their cause. However, others reasoned that the story gave the American public a better understanding of the problems of slavery and racism.

*

Another expression that originated in *Uncle Tom's Cabin* is **It Just Growed Like Topsy**, which is used to describe something that has appeared unexpectedly from nowhere and grown with extraordinary speed. This comes from a passage in the book where Aunt Ophelia asks Topsy, a little slave girl, about her family. The girl denies she has any family or even that she was actually born: 'I spect I just grow'd,' she says. 'Don't think nobody ever made me.'

To be **Whiter Than White** is to be seen as pure, innocent and virtuous, never implicated in any wrongdoing. The phrase has been in use since the end of the 16th century, being lifted directly from Shakespeare's poem *Venus and Adonis* (1593), which includes the line: 'Teaching the sheets a whiter hew than white'. It was popularized and used widely throughout the English-speaking world as the result of an advertising campaign during the 1950s by the washing powder manufacturer Persil.

A **Legend in Their Own Lifetime** refers to someone who has achieved a level of fame and respect and been recognized for it while they are still alive, rather than posthumously. This expression was first used by the author Lytton Strachey when he described Florence Nightingale in his book *Eminent Victorians* (1918).

Laugh, I Thought I Was Going to Die was originally said in appreciation of something very funny
indeed, although over time it has come to acquire
sarcastic overtones to indicate you were slightly taken
aback by a person's cheek or rudeness. The expression passed into regular use thanks to an Albert
Chevalier song 'Knocked 'Em in the Old Kent Road',
popular in the Victorian music halls. But the origin
is thought to be found in Jane Austen's *Pride and
Prejudice* (1813), in which Lydia Bennet remarks:
'Lord! How I laughed . . . I thought I should have
died.' Over the years, the expression has been
modified and expanded to include: 'Laugh, I could
have cried', 'Laugh, I nearly started' and my personal
favourite: 'Laugh? I was laughing, my mate, he was
laughing, they were all laughing over there too'.

THAT'S ENTERTAINMENT

To **Box and Cox** means to alternate between two situations simultaneously, usually in a half-hearted manner and often with disastrous consequences. *Box and Cox – A Romance of Real Life in One Act* is the title of a play by John Maddison Morton, first produced at the Royal Lyceum Theatre in London on 1 November 1847. The play was so popular it was also turned into an opera in 1866 by Arthur Sullivan (of Gilbert and Sullivan fame) and performed again in the 1920s in a new production by the D'Oyly Carte Opera Company. The story tells of John Box and James Cox, two men who were renting the very same room from an unscrupulous landlady, Mrs Bouncer. One of the men worked all day long and the other all night, so were quite unaware of the presence of each other in the room, although they did meet twice a day on the stairs. Eventually the deception is revealed and, in a farcical scene, the two men then play dice for the room. The whole episode ends happily with the discovery that they are, in fact, long-lost brothers.

Running the **Whole Gamut of Emotions** is an unusual expression used to describe the full range between delirious joy and abject misery. There is a simple musical explanation for the word. The original musical scale, devised by Guido d'Arezzo during the 11th century, used letters of the Greek alphabet. The lowest note in the vocal scale was called 'gamma' (the third letter in the alphabet) and the highest note was called 'ut'. Therefore 'gamma' and 'ut' came together to describe the entire musical range. These days children use 'doh, ray, me', etc., to sing out the musical scale, and once again our language has a great deal to thank the Greeks for. Can you imagine running the whole 'doh-doh' of emotions? (I guess Homer Simpson probably could.)

To give a **Barnstorming** performance is to execute something in a particularly exhilarating fashion – such as a public speaker delivering a rousing speech, or an actor or musician thrilling an audience. However, the original barnstormers were just second-rate thespians who toured the American countryside in the early 19th century, performing to locals in a barn. These actors were famous for their exaggerated style, often producing rousing theatre (akin to the fury of a storm) in order to compensate for their lack of dramatic skill. The expression passed over into wider use thanks to the US politicians of the time who hijacked the actors' style and toured the states giving stirring, excitable speeches, typically also in barns, in an effort to win votes. The phrase was also applied to the early aviators; particularly stunt pilots who would perform hair-raising flights for a fee.

To **Ham It Up** or be a **Ham Actor** is taken to apply to an amateur or unskilled thespian, a jobbing actor who remains largely unknown and only ever has the bit parts in a play. This reference first appeared in print in 1882 and was directed at the travelling black and white minstrel shows in America. It is often suggested the term was immortalized by these popular shows and there is some evidence to support this. The famous entertainers used to perform a ballad called 'The Ham-Fat Man', which is said to refer to low-paid actors who used ham fat to remove their stage make-up after a show. Apparently the phrase was later shortened to 'ham' and directed at any substandard performer. Hence boxers who display little dexterity are known as **Ham-fisted**, an expression extended to fumbling attempts at just about anything. Also, amateur radio enthusiasts who enjoy tuning in and broadcasting goodness knows what to each other, are still called **Radio Hams**.

A second theory suggests the phrase relates directly to a 19th-century actor named Hamish

McCulloch, who was nicknamed 'Ham' and led a troupe of travelling performers called 'The Ham Actors' who toured Illinois in the 1880s giving less than impressive performances. But the expression in fact pre-dates all of the above by some 280 years. In his play *Troilus and Cressida* (1601), William Shakespeare writes (in Act 1, Scene iii):

> *And, like a strutting player, whose conceit*
> *Lies in his hamstring and doth think it rich*
> *To hear the wooden dialogue and sound*
> *'Twixt his stretch'd footing and the scaffoldage . . .*

Here Shakespeare is suggesting how a 'wooden' actor might over-compensate by stretching his hamstring and pointing his foot towards the stage, in ballerina fashion. In fact, from contemporary engravings, it looks like most of the old Bard's players did just that.

But this is all a bit vague for me. For a more solid explanation we need to go back over a hundred years to the American Deep South and to a particular interpretation of the Bible. The Old Testament tells us how Ham's son Canaan was punished by God and forced to work as a servant (or slave) to his brothers. In America during the 1800s, black slaves became known as 'sons of Ham' in reference to their lowly status. Indeed there was a widespread belief at the time that, according to the Bible, all black people were descendants of Ham and therefore *should* be treated as slaves. There is good evidence to support the fact that this is the derivation of the word 'ham' as applied to sub-standard performers and performances, although the expression is not meant as unkindly today as it was when first used in the southern states of America all those years ago.

Hell Hath No Fury Like a Woman Scorned is a popular and expressive phrase indicating that a woman, when deceived by her lover, will be so incensed that she'll do anything to get her own back, however violent or destructive. The full line comes from William Congreve's play *The Mourning Bride* (1607): 'Heaven has no rage, like love to hatred turned,/Nor hell a fury, like a woman scorned.' He might well be right, but isn't it about time those furious women got over it and moved on for the peace of the rest of us? (See also **Bunny Boiler**.)

It's a Funny Old World is an expression we are all prone to using at one time or another to indicate an acceptance of a situation, albeit reluctantly, but it can also be used to express an unexpected stroke of good fortune. It is a phrase lifted directly from the film world and in particular the movie *You Are Telling Me* (1934), starring W. C. Fields. At one point the great man states: 'It's a funny old world, a man is lucky if he gets out of it alive.' The tongue-in-cheek humour of the line was enough for it to be repeated all over the land as soon as the film was released and become established as part of the

English language. In 1990, the British prime minister, Margaret Thatcher, was reported to have said, with tears in her eyes at the cabinet meeting where she was ousted as leader: 'It's a funny old world, isn't it.' (It was a moment that certainly had me laughing.)

To **Know Where All the Bodies Are Buried** puts a person in a very strong position with their employers as it means they know all the inner secrets of an organization, and this may be damaging if that person should ever leave to join a rival company. Mainly an American expression, this is none the less used widely in business circles in Britain. It derives from the cult American movie *Citizen Kane* (1941), which was produced and directed by, as well as starring, Orson Welles. In one famous scene, Susan Alexander, Kane's estranged wife, remarks of the butler at Xanadu: 'but he knows where all the bodies are buried'. The phrase immediately caught on and has been particularly popular on both sides of the Atlantic since the cut-throat business boom of the 1980s.

To have the **Heebie Jeebies** is to be in a state of high anxiety and fear. There have been some suggestions over the years that this expression has a racial overtone and is in some way connected to the anti-Semitic word 'Hebe', a derogatory term for 'Hebrew' (i.e. a Jew). However, nothing could be further from the truth. The source of this phrase lies in fact in the work of the popular American cartoonist William (Billy) De Beck, where it was used to mean 'the frights'. Making his debut in 1919, in the sports section of the *Chicago Herald and Examiner* as 'Take Barney Google, F'rinstance', 'Barney Google' was a little chap with big eyes who was involved in boxing and horse racing. In 1924, De Beck introduced a new character, a racehorse called 'Spark Plug', leading to a huge increase in the popularity of the strip, which by then was being syndicated all over America. In 1934, De Beck had his two main characters, Barney and Spark Plug, trek to the North Carolina mountains where they met a new favourite called Snuffy Smith, a moonshiner (see **Moonlight Flit**) involved in the illegal distilling and selling of alcohol during the Prohibition. The comic strip focused attention on the narrow-minded, stereotypical attitudes of hillbillies in southern Appalachia, where locals were suspicious of outsiders, or 'flatlanders', and the Federal Revenue agents, or 'revenooers'. Barney Google now appears across 21 countries in 11 different languages and has been credited with introducing several slang phrases, including 'sweet mama', 'horsefeathers' and 'hotsie-totsie', in addition to 'heebie-jeebies', although only the latter remains in regular use today, 80 years after it first appeared in print.

In 1995, the strip was one of 20 featured in the 'Comic Strip Classic' series of commemorative American postage stamps, and it is also credited for the origin of the phrase **Googly Eyed**. In 1998, Larry Page and Sergei Brin formed the software company Google, which provides a search facility for the World Wide Web, and they based their company's name on the mathematical term 'googol', which represents the number ten followed by 100 zeros. Back in 1940, a mathematician named Edward Kasner asked his nine-year-old nephew, Milton Sirotta, to think of a name for such a large number. Apparently the boy immediately came up with the word 'googol', which Kasner liked and assigned the term to the value of ten to the googol power. A nine-year-old boy and one of the most popular cartoon characters of the time called Barney Google? I can see a connection there.

Drinking at the Last Chance Saloon indicates that someone has run out of options and that now is the time to produce results, before it's too late. Usually a media term, the phrase can often be heard at the home of all silly clichés, the football world, where a player or team might be so described when being offered their very last opportunity to improve. The source of this expression is probably the old westerns where the Last Chance Saloon was the inn at the end of town, the final chance for cowboys, outlaws and rustlers to have a good drink before riding off into the remote, sun-drenched, dusty plain – and no doubt falling off and discovered later proposing marriage to a cactus plant. The phrase became popular thanks to a famous Marlene Dietrich song in the film *Destry Rides Again* (1939). Most writers and authors find themselves in the Last Chance Saloon at one time or another but, readers be assured, it is much more fun in there than it is in the No Chance Saloon.

A **Damp Squib** is something of an anticlimax. Many a time we look forward to an event with great enthusiasm only to be let down and disappointed. A 'squib' is a small firework thrown by hand, and a damp one is hardly likely to excite anybody awaiting the loud pops and bangs of proper fireworks. They are bound to be disappointed.

To **Lay It on with a Trowel** is to be especially generous with your flattery and praise. The expression is thought to have been invented by the two-times British prime minister Benjamin Disraeli, who said of the royal family, when speaking to Matthew Arnold: 'Everyone likes flattery and when you come to Royalty you should lay it on with a trowel.' (No wonder he was such a successful Tory leader.) However, the origin can be found in Shakespeare's *As You Like It* (1598), where the Bard describes flattery being 'slapped on thick and without nicety, like mortar'.

To **Laugh Like a Drain** means to laugh out loud in an uncontrollable manner. The phrase is British in origin, dating to just after the Second World War, and reflects the echoing gurgle often heard emanating from the sewers and drains beneath the City of London.

Life Is Just a Bowl of Cherries, used to describe everything that is wonderful with our lives, is hardly one of our most profound expressions, but it is still a popular one, especially in the North of England. It is a comparatively modern proverb, which originates from the musical *Scandals*, first produced in America in 1919, which included a popular song entitled 'Life is Just a Bowl of Cherries', by George Gershwin.

When a person is not keen to tell us where they are going, they may instead remark they are **Off to See a Man About a Dog**. During the age of the Victorian music hall and theatre, a popular play called *Flying Scud* (1866) by Dion Boucicault (one of the most successful playwrights of the 19th century), was produced first in London and then opened in New York soon afterwards. Whenever the lead character found himself in an awkward situation, he would take his leave by announcing he 'had to see a man about a dog'. Audiences found this very funny, and people were soon copying the expression on both sides of the Atlantic to explain their whereabouts.

*

To be **Made of Sterner Stuff** is to be strong both mentally and emotionally, having firm resolve and not buckling easily under pressure. Once again, we turn to the inventive prose of William Shakespeare for the origin of this phrase. In his play *Julius Caesar* (1599), Mark Antony, when speaking at Caesar's funeral, responds to the claim that he is ruthless and determined: 'Did this in Caesar seem ambitious? When that the poor have cried, Caesar hath wept; Ambition should be made of sterner stuff.' Subsequently, the expression has been in regular use all over the English-speaking world and popularized via literature.

The **World Is Your Oyster** would suggest to a person that anything is possible and that hard work and careful decisions will lead to great success in the future. It comes, like so many other phrases, from Shakespeare. In his play *The Merry Wives of Windsor* (1597), there is an exchange between Falstaff and Pistol in Act 2, Scene ii:

FALSTAFF: I will not lend thee a penny.
PISTOL: Why then, the world is mine oyster,
    Which I with sword shall open.

To **Muff** something is to make an easy mistake or, in the context of sport, to fail to catch a ball. The word can also be applied to the person involved, who is perceived as awkward, clumsy and dull. It has been in use for centuries and possibly originates from a play called *The Rival Candidates* (1774) in which the character Sir Harry Muff appears as a clumsy, blundering old fool. 'Muff' became more widely recognized and used, particularly by schoolboys, as a result of Thomas Hughes' *Tom Brown's Schooldays* (1857), which regularly includes the word, as in: 'I didn't think, madam, that you would have been such a muff as to let him be getting wet through at this time of day.'

'Muff' has been applied in other ways too over the years. For example, in Ireland the word has been used to indicate a flat or level plain, and there are still several towns and villages going by the name of Muff. Eglinton, for instance, when it was founded in 1619 by the Grocers' Company of London, was originally called Muff until its name was changed in 1858 in honour of the 13th Earl of Eglinton. In Sweden, *muff* means 'sleeve', which in turn derives from the Dutch word *mof*, and is also the name given to a woollen hand warmer that hangs down at about waist height, suspended from a cord around the neck. Fashionable women all over Scandinavia were soon getting out their muffs on cold days to keep their hands warm, and the fashion spread to England. These hand warmers are still used in Scandinavia, and ladies often now slip a small chemically powered heating element into their muffs for added warmth. This is also where the term **Ear Muffs** originates.

EXOTIC ORIGINS

The **Abominable Snowman** is a popular name given to a Yeti, the large man-like beast said to be living in the Himalayas. As a kid, I could never understand why, as 'abominable' means 'causing moral revulsion'. And my snowmen never did that; they were happy fellows with carrot noses, proudly wearing my old Chelsea scarf. When I set about finding out why, I discovered a Tibetan legend describing the Yeti as a fearsome creature with a near-human face that would raid remote mountain villages. The story was spread by the early European mountaineers attempting to conquer Mount Everest in the 1920s. By the 1950s, the legend was firmly established and enhanced by both Nicholas Blake's detective novel *The Case of the Abominable Snowman* (1941) and the film *The Abominable Snowman*, released in 1957. In the 1960s, the first man to reach the summit of

Everest, Sir Edmund Hillary, claimed to have found large bear-like footprints when he was there in 1953, which only added to the legend. But why is it abominable? The answer can be found in the Tibetan word for Yeti, *Meetohkangmi* – *meetoh* meaning 'foul' and *kangmi* 'snowman'. Clearly Nicholas Blake had understood the translation when he thought up the title of his book.

An **Assassin** is a paid mercenary, a person who is prepared to kill another for a fee. Although sometimes they will eliminate a powerful or important figure, usually political, for free. The original assassins were a group of Muslim fanatics who came together in Persia around 1090. Their leader was one Hasan-e Sabbah who himself died in 1124. Their main targets were members of the ruling Seljuk authority, who controlled vast areas between Persia and Iraq and had extended their empire into Syria by the 12th century. For generations they had been directing murderous and violent attacks against their ruling administrations, usually after fuelling themselves with hashish. This is how they became known, and feared, as the *Hashashshin* or 'Hashish eaters'.

*

To **Run Amock**, or **Run Amuck** (depending upon your preference), means to be in a wild, frenzied state and out of control. Such behaviour can now be witnessed in most English high streets of a weekend evening. Although I doubt any of those involved would know the expression derives from the Malaysian word *amoq* which, literally translated, describes the behaviour of tribesmen who, under the influence of opium, would become wild, rampaging mobs attacking anybody in their path. The phrase became well known in England during the 17th century when the great travellers-turned-writers of the day would show off their knowledge of far-away cultures by including such terms in their prose and poetry. Three hundred years later, the phrase was firmly established in the West. It appears, for instance, in P. G. Wodehouse's *Uncle Fred in Springtime* (1939): 'So that when the policeman arrived and found me running amuck with an assegai, apparently without provocation, it was rather difficult to convince him that I wasn't drunk.' I doubt Wodehouse was high on opium either when he wrote this. (An assegai is a lance or javelin, by the way.)

Vandalism is something almost every town is affected by, unfortunately, due to the useless, mindless idiots who enjoy breaking up and damaging anything they see, all in the name of fun. The original useless, mindless idiots were a Teutonic race whose presence was initially recorded in northeastern Germany throughout the fifth and sixth centuries and who were known as the Vandals. First they ransacked France (Gaul) in the latter part of the fourth century, followed by Spain in 409, Africa in 429 and, led by King Genseric, they then headed for Rome in 455 where they destroyed public monuments, works of art and literature, just for the fun of it. The original use of the word 'vandalism' was to describe the wilful and unnecessary destruction of works of art, although these days our modern street vandals wouldn't recognize a work of art if it jumped up and down in front of them and slapped them in the face. So instead they stick with what they know best: burger bars, cars, the housing estate they themselves live on and isolated shopping precincts. Not quite Rome and Africa, but as cultured as we can expect hooligans in Middle England to be these days. Although there was another group who also invaded Spain in the fifth century who called themselves the 'Alans'. Perhaps that is what we should call the modern-day English version, especially as they would only confuse it with cockney rhyming slang 'the Alans' (Alan Whickers – knickers).

When we are **Down in the Dumps** we are feeling low in spirits and thinking that perhaps life is passing us by. This expression started life as 'in the doleful dumps' and can be connected to the Dutch word *domp*, which can be translated as 'hazy' or 'doleful'. The phrase has been in use since the Anglo-Dutch wars of the mid to late 17th century and crops up repeatedly in Samuel Pepys's *Diary*.

When you are offered something that is **Buckshee**, you should be quite pleased as it means it is free of charge. Some authorities believe this to be a piece of cockney rhyming slang for 'free', although in fact the word is lifted from the days our English soldiers served in India under the British Raj. The original Persian word *baksheesh* can be translated as 'gratuity' or 'tip'.

Stemming the Flow of blood or water is one of the most commonly used phrases and it doesn't even occur to many of us that it is actually an idiom. One of the oldest in our language, the expression can be traced back to the Viking invasions of the late eighth century and the old Nordic language they brought along with them. The Vikings used to build dams and the Norse word for one of those is *stemma*, which, loosely translated, means to 'dam up' or 'stop'. The word soon became a part of our everyday language and remained so, even after we had managed to finally stemma the flow of Vikings across the North Sea.

The phrase **Blood Is Thicker Than Water** suggests that family bonds of trust and loyalty are stronger than those friendships we make for ourselves. I for one have never believed this, and was unable to work out the 'water' connection until I started to look at the many biblical references to the phrase. In ancient Middle Eastern culture, blood rituals symbolized bonds that were far greater than those of the family. Hence the bond between **Blood Brothers** – warriors who symbolically share the blood they have shed together in battle – is far stronger than the one between you and the boy you grew up with who kept pinching your records. In addition, there is an expression dating back three thousand years that tells us: 'The blood of the covenant is far stronger than the water of the womb', which is a forerunner of the phrase we use today. In modern times, we understand 'blood' to be the bloodline of a family, but, as you can see, that is not the original meaning of the expression at all. Its meaning has thus been corrupted over the centuries, probably by the English nobility of the Middle Ages to whom the 'blood line' was all important.

*

SHAGGY DOGS AND BLACK SHEEP

Filthy Lucre is a phrase used to describe ill-gotten gains. The word 'lucre' derives from the Latin word *lucrum*, meaning 'profit', 'gain', 'greed' or 'wealth', and other similar Greek words for 'stolen goods'. The 'filthy' part has just been added to reinforce the idea of 'dirty' (i.e. stolen) money. The Hindi word *lut*, translated as 'stolen money', is pronounced **Loot** by Indian people, which is how that word became part of our criminal slang during the 1800s.

To take a sharp blow in the **Goolies** can bring a tear to a gentleman's eye and quite ruin his afternoon. (It is no laughing matter.) This slang expression first became used in England during the 1930s as an inoffensive and comical way of describing a man's pride and joy. Queen Victoria's army, who, in the name of empire building, went off to make new friends around the world at the point of their bayonets in an attempt to paint the world map red, brought this expression back from India with them in the mid 1800s. Quite simply, the Hindustani word for 'balls' is *goolies*.

When something is **Blown to Smithereens** it has been shattered into thousands of small pieces. This expression is of Gaelic origin, 'smithereens' meaning 'small or tiny fragments'. The Gaelic spelling of the word is *smidirín*, which leads us to a modern Irish expression for severe hangovers, which I understand are quite common over there. To **Be in Schmids** (in pieces) is the evocative phrase used on the Emerald Isle to express such a sorry state of affairs.

To **Butter Someone Up** is to flatter them with smooth talk. Some suggest this is linked with the smooth way butter spreads on to bread, to make it more palatable. We might continue to believe this until we visited the Hindu temple in Madurai, Tamil Nadu (supposedly the largest temple in the world), where guides speak of the ancient custom of throwing butterballs of ghee (the clarified butter used as the basis of all Indian cooking) at the statues of gods, a method of seeking favour by 'buttering up the gods'. We also know that during celebrations for the Tibetan New Year, the lamas at all the monasteries create 'butter flowers' or sculptures out of coloured butter. These are then traditionally displayed on the 15th day of the Tibetan lunar year following a religious ceremony the previous evening. The tradition of creating butter sculptures, to worship statues of Buddha, can be traced to the Tang Dynasty (AD 618–907) and the belief that such offerings would bring peace and happiness for the full lunar year. This tradition was known as 'buttering up the Buddha'.

The phrase **Has the Cat Got Your Tongue?** is used when a normally talkative person suddenly has little or nothing to say about a subject, perhaps out of guilt. There are two possible origins for this expression and we know that it was originally recorded in print in 1911. The first suggestion is that the cat in question is the cat o' nine tails (see **You Scratch My Back and I'll Scratch Yours**) and that the hapless victim would be rendered speechless by the punishment imposed. A slight extension to this is the idea that if the captain or his officers discussed any official secrets then the punishment for revealing them to others would be flogging with the 'cat'. Others would consider them too afraid to speak and suggested the 'cat had hold of their tongue'.

The version I favour, however, can be traced back to many years before England ruled the waves. In the Middle East, it was a traditional punishment during medieval times – a custom that dated back to 500 BC – for liars and blasphemers to have their tongues cut out and then fed to the cats. The ancient Egyptians were the first to keep domestic cats and used them to control vermin and other pests that infested their food stores. These voracious felines were known to eat anything, including human tongues, which even the dogs would turn their noses up at. In ancient Egypt, the cat was also revered as a hunter and even worshipped as a deity. Therefore feeding them the tongues of liars was seen as a human offering to the gods.

*

Having a Yen for something is an American phrase
– although often used in the British ports of London,
Liverpool and Glasgow – which expresses a great
desire or longing. The yen in question is surpris-
ingly not the Japanese currency, but a reference to
Chinese opium, a drug freely available in both
Britain and America during the late 1800s, and the
opium dens that proliferated in Victorian back
streets and were regularly frequented by Sherlock
Holmes in Sir Arthur Conan Doyle's stories of the
famous detective. The phrase comes from the
Chinese word *yan*, which can be translated as
'craving'.

The word **Quiz** is worth recording because of the
wonderful story surrounding its origin. Quiz nights
in pubs and clubs throughout the world are as popular today as they ever have been, but to find the
source of the word we must travel to Dublin. During
the 1700s, a man called Daly was the manager of a
theatre in the centre of the city. In 1780, he made a
wager with friends one evening that he could introduce a brand new word, with no meaning at all, to
the English language, and what's more he said he
could do it within 48 hours. The bet was accepted
and within hours Daly had chalked the letters
Q-U-I-Z on doors and walls all over the city. The
word immediately became the centre of attention
and within weeks newspapers were running features
on what it may possibly mean. Daly won his bet

because the word became associated with asking questions and finding answers, with people mulling over the 'quiz' question in coffee houses and inns throughout Ireland and England. Unfortunately, there is no hard evidence to support the truth of this story, but it is still a good one and is often repeated by trivia enthusiasts.

To **See Naples and Die** is actually an old Italian expression, one that has filtered through into the English language, albeit meaning something entirely different. The suggestion was that there was no place more beautiful on earth than Naples and that once you had been there then nothing else on the planet was worth seeing. They would have you believe you had experienced Utopia. The phrase was first recorded in 1787 when the German writer Johann Wolfgang von Goethe wrote, of Naples, in his book *Italian Journey*: 'I will not say another word about the beauties of the city and its situation, which have been described and praised so often. As they say here *"Vedi Napoli e poi muori"*', meaning 'see Naples and die'. But the expression has become far more ominous over the years – 'see Naples and (literally) die' – and points to the time when the city was a notorious centre for cholera, typhoid and many other deadly diseases, which might explain how the phrase became better known among English travellers.

*

A **Tea Caddy** is a place we store our tea leaves or tea bags. Well, at least our grandparents did. The phrase derives from the Malaysian word *kati* for the measurement, slightly over a pound, of tea traditionally sold throughout Southeast Asia. A 'tea-*kati*' would be what was brought home from the market. The popular idiom used for an errand boy, or something that 'carries', could also have something to do with the expression (see also **Caddy**).

The **Whole Kit and Caboodle**, an expression mainly used in America, has to be one of our more unusual idioms. We understand it to mean 'absolutely everything', 'the whole lot'. The word 'caboodle' comes from the Dutch word *boedel*, which means 'possessions', while kit has been a short word used for 'equipment' for centuries. Collectively the 'whole kit and caboodle' has meant 'everything you have in your possession' since the first Dutch settlers arrived in the New World in the 17th century with all their boodle.

THIS SPORTING LIFE

When we are **Rooting for Someone** we are right behind everything they do and wanting them to succeed. The expression has its foundation in American slang from around the turn of the 19th/20th century. It originates from the sports stadiums where supporters would urge on their teams by singing, cheering and generally causing uproar. Quite possibly, the reason we are 'rooting' for somebody could be a corruption of the phrase 'to rout', meaning 'to cause uproar'.

To **Blow the Gaff** is to reveal a secret of some sort or to inform on a person. At carnivals and fairgrounds during the 18th century, unscrupulous operators would use a concealed device in games in order to reduce a customer's chance of winning. In carnival slang this was known as a 'gaff'. It is also recorded that around that time the word 'blow' was slang for 'reveal' or 'expose' and therefore to expose the hidden deception at the carnival became known as 'blowing the gaff', which was in regular use in England by 1812.

There are many interesting uses of the word 'blow' that mean little in translation. Take, for example, 'to blow a raspberry'. This is 19th-century slang describing a show of contempt by making a rude noise and it was popular with audiences in the Victorian comedy theatres. The phrase is easily explained by the colourful cockney rhyming slang, which tells us that 'blowing a raspberry tart' can be used in place of the word 'fart'. Also, there are many that are more easily explained, such as 'blowing a kiss', 'blow away the cobwebs', 'blowing your brains out', 'blowing your mind', 'blowing over', 'blowing your socks off', 'blow your top', 'blow me tight' and 'blowing my horn'. Perhaps it is time to move on.

To be **Blackballed** is to be excluded from a club or society by other members who vote against an application for membership. That can also be extended to being left out of any social event or gathering. The phrase became known in 1770 when the practice of 'balling' was adopted by the London gentlemen's clubs. The idea was that if a new member was proposed, then every existing member of the club would be asked if he had any objection to the new addition to their apparently elite and sought-after group. After all, it wouldn't do at all for a gentleman to find himself sitting at the table next to a sworn enemy, as that could quite spoil a chap's luncheon. Instead, members were asked to place a white or black ball anonymously into a symbolic urn or bag. One single black ball was enough to refuse a membership and nobody at the club would ever know who had opposed the application.

Although the phrase had been in use throughout London society for centuries, it became better known to the rest of us when the BBC journalist and *Newsnight* presenter Jeremy Paxman was turned down by the Garrick Club in 1993 after being black-balled by unknown members who were enraged by his anti-establishment book *Friends in High Places* (1991). But it works both ways. Groucho Marx famously responded, when invited to join an exclusive club: 'Thank you but *no* thank you. I would never join a club that would have somebody like me as a member.' It was quite a relief, I can assure you, to discover that 'balling' in gentlemen's clubs was only a membership issue.

This process of balling provides us with another, apparently unconnected, expression, which is to be **Pipped at the Post**, meaning to be beaten at the last moment. The allusion is that during a race another competitor could overtake the leader right at the winning post, which is certainly how the phrase became so regularly used, especially within the racing fraternity. But this word 'pipped' didn't make sense until I started looking a little further into what it means. The 'black ball' used in the voting procedure was originally called a 'pip', named after the black olive stones that were used centuries earlier when the Greeks and later the Romans voted on social issues. Apparently if only a single black pip (black ball) was found to have been cast, then the proposed issue had been 'pipped' (narrowly defeated). That phrasing was then taken by latter generations to the race track.

A **Blue Ribbon Event** is the one of the highest distinction or prominence. In Britain the highest award for merit is a knighthood, usually bestowed by the sovereign either to honour great achievement or given to those who donate the most money to the governing political party of the time. Foremost among the orders of knighthood is the Most Noble Order of the Garter, so called because of the garter of dark blue velvet ribbon worn by recipients. None of this is of any particular interest, at least not to me; however, it does provide the background to why we use it in describing a prestigious sporting event. In 1846, Lord George Bentinck gave up racing to pursue a political career, selling all his horses and becoming leader of the Conservative Party in the process. As things turned out, Bentinck was defeated in Parliament in 1848 and only a few days afterwards, on 28 May, Surplice, one of the horses he had recently sold, won the Derby, the most prestigious of all horse-racing events. Bentinck was distraught and the great Benjamin Disraeli later recalled in his autobiography an exchange he had with his friend, the Tory leader, in the library of the House of Commons:

'All my life I have been trying for this, and for what have I sacrificed it?' he murmured.

It was in vain to offer solace.

'You do not know what the Derby is,' he moaned out.

'Yes I do, it is the blue ribbon of the turf.'

'It is the blue ribbon of the turf,' he slowly repeated to himself, and sitting down at the table he buried himself in a folio of statistics.

To this day the Epsom Derby is still known as *the* blue ribbon event.

A **Below the Belt** remark can be considered a little offensive, insensitive and not in keeping with the spirit of matters. In 1867, the Marquis of Queensberry produced a set of rules to govern the sport of boxing, as prior to this 'professional' fights were nothing more than a lawless brawl. One of the rules Queensberry introduced was that 'no boxer must ever aim a blow at an opponent below the level of his trouser belt'. If a boxer did, then that would be considered an unsporting gesture and the victim would be given 'as much time as he needs to recover'. Presumably, before 1867, all fighters were allowed to punch opponents in the Bow Locks area.

To **Call a Person's Bluff** is to test their claims and issue a challenge for them to reveal the truth. Poker, from which the phrase derives, is essentially a game of deception where each player pretends to have the winning hand and the others have to consider the truth of that assertion against the value of the cards in their own hand. Once play begins, the chips (money tokens) are placed on the table and then the **Chips Are Down** (things are getting serious). The expression **Poker Faced**, meaning to reveal no outward emotion, comes from this part of the game. Some players, suspecting others have a superior hand by the way they are **Upping the Stakes** (putting more chips on the table) may pass their cards back to the dealer, face down, so the others won't know how they have been betting. This is known as 'folding the cards' and a player who does this has **Folded**, as a business might these days when it ceases to trade. However, at any point players can pay more money into the 'pot' (hence **Gone to Pot**) and call another person's 'bluff' by paying them to reveal their cards (**Put Their Cards on the Table**). Finally, if something is very likely to happen, and can be foreseen, it might be thought of as being **On the Cards**. But this expression has nothing to do with poker; instead it relates to the practice of fortune telling and reading tarot cards. The phrase has been in regular use from the early 1800s both in England and across Europe since the practice originated in Italy sometime between 1440 and 1450.

A **Blue Chip Company**, or a **Blue Chip Investment**, is considered to be the most sought after and reliable. In gaming houses and casinos across the world, players never use cash to gamble with. Instead, they lodge their money with a cashier in exchange for chips, so called because they were originally chips of wood, coloured in accordance with their value. These days they are mass-produced plastic discs, although still known as gaming chips. The blue-coloured chips were initially the highest in value and consequently the most popular and secure.

When a person is having **High Jinks**, they will be lively and excited – basically having a good time. This term has a Scottish origin and can be traced to the late 1800s and early 1900s when drinking parties at the great houses north of the Border were at their most decadent. During this time there was one popular game where dice were thrown to see who among the group would have to drink a huge and potent cocktail which was likely to have the loser ricocheting along the corridors in no time at all. Then the dice would be thrown again and the loser this time would pay for the drink. Walter Scott in his novel *Guy Mannering* (1815) stated how 'high jinx' was the term used for this sort of forfeit game, although not a drinking game: 'The frolicsome company had begun to practise the ancient and now forgotten pastime of High Jinx. This game was played in several ways. Most frequently the company threw the dice and those upon whom the lot fell were obliged to assume and maintain for a certain time, a certain fictitious character or to repeat a certain number.'

An **Ace in the Hole** is a well-known cliché used to suggest a hidden advantage or a secret source of influence. It is an American phrase that was used as the title of a Cole Porter song in one of his shows, *Let's Face It*, in 1941. It was also the title of a Billy Wilder film, first screened in 1951. The phrase, echoed in England as an **Ace Up His Sleeve**, originated during the 1920s in the popular card game stud poker. The rules state that after each round of betting, every player (of which there can be up to ten) is dealt one more card face upwards with the exception of the last player, who is dealt a card face downwards, known as the 'hole card'. The winner of the game is determined by whoever has either the highest- or the lowest-scoring hand, and the two share the pot (the winnings). An ace in the 'hole' (or up your sleeve) is obviously a huge and hidden advantage to a gambler.

When something **Comes Up Trumps** it is an unexpected positive result, right at the last minute. Many popular card games are played with trump cards in the pack. The word 'trump' is an anglicized version of the French word *triomphe*, meaning 'triumphant'. In most card games, a trump card is a valuable one to hold; hence if a player with a poor hand, facing defeat, draws a trump card at the last moment, their luck might well turn around.

To **Turn the Tables** on a person is to reverse the situation or conditions completely. This expression derives from the old practice, during board games such as draughts or chess, of actually turning the board around once you were in a dominant position, to see if you could still beat an opponent from the disadvantaged position they themselves had been in.

When the shout of **Fore** goes up on a golf course, everybody who hears it ducks for fear of receiving a golf ball in the back of their head. The word is usually misunderstood as 'four' but the correct spelling leads us to the root of the expression. The word 'fore', especially in nautical parlance, has always meant something that is ahead, or in front. It has been prefixed to many other words over the years, giving us foremen, forearms, forerunners, fore-thought, foremost, foresee, foretell, forestall and others. There is no certain origin for the word, but there are two stories well worth recording. Some researchers suggest the term can be traced to the British infantrymen who would shout the word before firing as a warning to those ahead of them, which is a little strange because you would assume they were aiming at those ahead of them in the first place. However, it is known that John Knox, the 16th-century 'hellfire preacher', was quoted as saying: 'One among many comes to the East Port of Leith, where lay two great pieces of ordnance, and where their enemies were known to be, and cried to his fellows that were at the gate making defence: "War Before!" and so fires one great piece, and thereafter the other.'

Ramsey's Fort in Leith directly overlooked the Leith Links Golf Course at the time, so it is entirely possible gunners would use the cry to warn golfers of impending target practice from the fort walls. It is thus easy to see how golfers would use the same expression when warning other players of a ball heading in their direction. Robert Clark, writing in

1875, suggested the second possibility by drawing attention to Andrew Dickenson, the first recorded caddy, who was carrying the clubs of the Duke of York in 1681 and whom he describes as a 'fore-caddy'. They were the boys who would wait ahead in the fairway and spot a golfer's ball as it landed. It is also easy to see how they might be warned of a ball heading towards them with the shout of 'fore-caddy', combining the words 'fore' and 'caddy'. And this leads us to the origin of the word **Caddy**.

The word is first recorded in Scotland in 1610 and derives from the French word *cadet*, meaning 'junior' (in rank or position). It appears that cadets, or junior soldiers, would carry the clubs of the golfing royalty and senior military men, and it is very likely the term travelled to Scotland with Mary Stuart on her return in 1561. It is also known at that time the word 'caddy' was applied to many errand boys whose job it was to carry items such as the water-caddies (see also **Tea Caddy**). Before we leave the world of golf, we should also record the origin of the word Handicap, meaning 'disadvantage'. Quite simply, it derives from an old card game called 'hand I the cap'. Players would place their stake money into a cap, which was passed among the other players as they dealt the cards in their turn. If a dealer won his hand, he was able to raise the stakes, to the disadvantage of the next dealer in line, who received the 'hand I cap'. The first written record of the card game can be found in Samuel Pepys's *Diary* in the entry for 18 September 1680.

To **Have Another String to Your Bow** means having more than one skill or opportunity and not to limit yourself to just one possible course of action. This expression dates to the Middle Ages when archers would carry a second string attached to the top of their bows and wound around the handle. This meant that if their bowstring snapped, they were able to re-string the bow using the reserve bowstring, ensuring they were always able to defend themselves or to continue hunting.

To propose a toast with the words **Here's Mud in Your Eye** is generally regarded as a light-hearted and friendly gesture towards the other guests present and wishing good fortune to all. In fact, the expression started out as anything but good-natured and the origin can be traced to horse racing. To suggest others have 'mud in their eye' was originally meant to taunt your fellow competitors, as they would be behind your own horse in the race and therefore losing.

To find yourself in a **No Holds Barred** situation means no rules apply and that any measures may be taken to ensure a favourable outcome. This is a wrestling expression, similar to the **Gloves Are Off** in boxing, which also means that the rules of the

SHAGGY DOGS AND BLACK SHEEP

sport are being disregarded on this occasion. In wrestling, certain holds are banned because they are considered too dangerous. For example, strangle holds to the neck are banned, as is grabbing another wrestler's **Goolies** (see entry) until they submit. (See also **Below the Belt**.) However, in a contest where no holds are barred, anything goes.

To **Throw in the Towel** is to admit defeat and to give up on an idea completely. The expression was originally 'to throw in the sponge' and reflects the common practice during boxing matches, and bare-knuckle fighting, of a contestant's seconds accepting a defeat for their man by throwing in the sponge or towel, during a round, as a signal for the referee to stop the bout. It is an admission of defeat. A boxer's 'seconds' are his trainer and his cuts man, who will both enter the ring between rounds to tend to the fighter and provide encouragement. As each round begins, the match referee will announce 'seconds out', which is not, as sometimes believed, a counting down of the clock, but instead an instruction for the fighter's seconds to leave the ring.

To **Upset the Apple Cart** means to throw plans and intentions into confusion. During the 18th century, the 'apple cart' was a wrestling term for the upper body, and to 'upset the apple cart' meant to throw an opponent to the ground and scupper his chances of winning.

RELIGION

When the **Writing Is on the Wall** it means a particular, negative event is inevitable and virtually unavoidable. The Book of Daniel in the Bible tells the story of King Belshazzar who was feasting in Babylon while boasting about the power of his idols. God, on hearing this, diverted the River Euphrates so that Belshazzar's enemies could breach the walls of the city. As the king raised God's goblet high above his head, a hand appeared and wrote the words 'Mene, Mene, Tekel, Parsin', which translates as 'Numbered, Numbered, Weighed, Divided'. This was meant as a warning to the king of what was about to happen, but Belshazzar was uncertain of the meaning so he called upon Daniel to explain it to him. Daniel told Belshazzar that God had numbered the days left to him as king and that his reign was about to end. He told him he had been weighed in

God's scales, that his life had not measured up to God's standards and that his kingdom was to be divided up by his enemies, the Medes. It was a warning the Persians were about to invade and take over. For the king, the writing was well and truly on the wall.

Bread Is the Staff of Life is a famous 17th-century proverb illustrating the importance of bread as a staple of our daily diet. The phrase became popular after the publication in 1704 of Jonathan Swift's novel *Tale of a Tub* in which one character states: 'Bread . . . dear brothers, is the staff of life.' This is how the expression passed into common usage, but in fact bread has featured symbolically in all religions and is frequently mentioned throughout the Bible, such as in John 6:35: 'And Jesus said unto them, I am the bread of life: he that cometh to me shall never hunger.'

To take a person **Under Your Wing** is to provide them with friendly encouragement, advice and protection. The source of this expression, which has been in use for two millennia, can be traced to the Bible. In Matthew 23:37, Jesus expresses his sorrow at what has become of Jerusalem and declares his wish to protect his people, like a hen will protect her chicks by spreading her wings so that they can find safety and shelter beneath them: 'Oh Jerusalem, Jerusalem, thou that killest the prophets and stonest them which are sent unto thee. How often would I have garnered thy children together, even as a hen would gather her chickens under her wings, and ye would not!' After a speech like that, I really can't think why the people then turned their backs upon him. Maybe I will try it out myself on the streets of Woking tomorrow morning and see what happens.

A **Red Letter Day** is a day to be looked forward to and then remembered as a special one. In the old almanacs, and more often in the ecclesiastical calendars, saints' days and Christian festivals were printed in red ink and all others displayed in black ink. The 'red' days were the ones religious folk looked forward to the most as it meant a great feast and a party. In modern calendars, only Sundays and public holidays are printed in red, largely as a result of tradition and not because they mark any special events.

Ringing the Changes is an expression used when someone in authority is announcing variation, which tends to result in matters being carried out in much the same way as before. The source of this term can be found in the old English custom of bell ringing in the cathedrals and churches throughout the land. The 17th century brought about 'change ringing' ('changes' being the different order in which certain sets of bells can be rung). For example, a set of three can be rung in a series of 6 changes, a set of four can lead to 24 changes, a set of six has 720 changes, and so on, with the big belfries housing 12 bells capable of ringing 479,001,600 changes, which would take the best part of 38 years to complete.

If we are **Breaking Bread** together, we are sharing a meal and holding conversation in a congenial, open and friendly manner. This expression can be traced to the Last Supper when Jesus sat down with his disciples, broke a loaf of bread and shared it around with some wine. Not much of a party but it *was* the best they could expect in those days. In Paul's letter to the Corinthians, as later reported in the New Testament, 1.Cor.11:23, he describes the scene: 'the Lord Jesus, on the night he was betrayed, took a loaf of bread and when he had given thanks, he broke it and said, "This is my body that is for you."' Some 30 years later, Luke, agreeing with Paul's account, describes the same scene (Luke 22:19–20). This tradition has lasted for two thousand years, with the rite of the Eucharist being that part of the Christian Mass during which the bread is blessed, becoming the body of Christ, and is given to each member of the congregation. This is followed by wine, which is also blessed to become the blood of Christ. However, a small, dry wafer has now replaced bread for the service: they must be crackers.

*

Black Tuesday is a well-known expression used to describe 29 October 1929, which is the day panic set in at the New York Stock Exchange. But the Americans did not coin the phrase. A few years prior to that, on 15 April 1921, some trade unions in Britain ended their support for striking miners and, as a result, a general strike was narrowly avoided. Many in the Labour Movement regarded this as an unforgivable act of betrayal and the day became known to them as **Black Friday**. That is how the adjective 'black' began to be broadly used to describe an unforgettably bad day.

Since then we have had a **Black Wednesday**, the day after the US financial disaster in 1929, during which many traders and businessmen jumped out of their office windows to avoid the shame of financial ruin. (Those working on the ground floor had to find other ways!) In 1987, stock markets around the world crashed on 19 October, known as **Black Monday**, and a few days later we had a similar problem on **Black Thursday** (22 October). However, the original **Black Friday** is in fact Good Friday and the day of the Crucifixion. For two thousand years, religious folk have worn black on this day of mourning, hence the expression.

Ashes to Ashes and Dust to Dust is an expression used at every funeral service and has been for thousands of years. The ashes do not refer to the remains of a cremation, however, and the dust is nothing to do with a burial. Instead they relate to the practice, dating back to biblical times, of those in mourning, who sprinkled earth or sand (dust) and ashes over their heads at the funeral of a loved one. This was known to be an expression of an individual's own insignificance, worthlessness and personal humility in the presence of the deceased. The Book of Genesis (18:22) is responsible for starting it all off, with the lines: 'And Abraham answered and said, "Behold now, I have taken upon me to speak with the Lord, which am but dust and ashes."'

To achieve something by the **Skin of Your Teeth** is to do it by the narrowest of margins. This is a truly expressive phrase, which can be traced to the Bible, although it seems to have been misquoted somewhere along the way. The Book of Job (19:20) reads: 'My bone cleaveth to my skin and to my flesh and I am escaped with the skin of my teeth.' What this actually means was that all Job had left was the skin of his teeth; everything else had been taken from him, including his possessions, health, family and friends. But it is easy to see how that quotation can be misunderstood, and taken to mean that Job had narrowly escaped with his life. Misunderstood, but here to stay.

A **Wolf in Sheep's Clothing** is someone who is not quite what they appear to be at first glance. To begin with they might seem to be pleasant and friendly, but we soon detect a hidden menace. This expression, which has been much used over the centuries, can be found in one of Aesop's popular fables, dating back 1,400 years. The story tells of a wolf who wraps himself up in a sheep's fleece and sneaks past the shepherd, into the paddock, disguised as one of the flock. Once inside, he immediately eats up one of the lambs before his deception can be revealed. But the origin of the expression can be found in the Bible (Matthew 7:15), which states: 'Beware of false prophets, which come to you in sheep's clothing. Inwardly they are ravening wolves.'

The **Black Sheep of the Family** is generally regarded as a disgrace, different from the rest and with a rogue element implied. For thousands of years, a black lamb in a flock was always the unpopular one as its fleece could not be dyed and was therefore less valuable than those of the white lambs. Thomas Bastard (yes, his real name) wrote a poem, published in 1598, in which he presents the black sheep as a predator: 'Til now I thought the proverbe did but jest, which said a black sheepe was a biting beaste.' And in 1892 Rudyard Kipling included in one of his own poems the line 'Baa! Baa! Baa! – we're little black sheep who've gone astray.' While these poems brought the phrase into regular use in the English language, the expression can in fact be traced to the biblical shepherds who held the belief that a black-fleeced lamb was an unlucky omen and would always disturb the rest of the flock. Incidentally, such was Kipling's influence over his readers that he also introduced, through his poetry, other common expressions, including 'east is east, west is west', 'he travels fastest who travels alone' and 'the female of the species is more deadly than the male'.

When we sneeze in public, there is always somebody nearby, sometimes a complete stranger, who says '**Bless You**', but why? Research shows that, despite many variations, the common theme among all the possible sources is the medieval belief that sneezing expelled a person's soul from their living body, enabling an evil spirit or the devil to take possession instead. The only way for the 'clean' soul to return was to bless the person. It became a widely used phrase during the great plague of London in 1665 when sneezing was a symptom of the Black Death. Anybody sneezing surely needed blessing as their end was nigh.

A **Baptism of Fire** is a severe introduction to a new situation, such as a footballer's first game for a new club taking place during a hot-blooded cup final, or someone's first day in a new job coinciding with the busiest day of the year for that company. The actual phrase can be traced back as far as the mid 16th century and the purge by the Catholics of the heretic Christians who were martyred over the following century for their beliefs. And in horrific fashion too; by being burned at the stake. The Catholics had believed the Christians would learn of their lifetime 'crimes against God' at the gates of heaven and then be converted to Catholicism. Hence the sneering phrase 'this is your baptism, a baptism of fire'. The expression passed into wider use due to none other than Napoleon himself. While in exile on St Helena in 1817, Bonaparte is quoted as saying, 'I love a brave soldier who has undergone the "baptism of fire".' It seems to have been a family favourite as Napoleon III also used the term when he wrote to his wife shortly after the Battle of Saarbruck on 10 August 1870, proudly including details of their son's first experience of war: 'Louis has just received his baptism of fire.' Louis Bonaparte was just 14 years old at the time.

To **Play Devil's Advocate** is to be in the position of presenting a hypothetical argument to a suggestion or proposal. The source of this expression lies with the Catholic Church and the process of proposing a name for canonization, which is to make an individual into a saint. When a name is proposed, a member of the clergy is appointed to present the opposing argument and that person is known as the *advocatus diaboli*, from the Latin words *advocatus*, meaning 'summoned one', and *diaboli*, 'of the devil'. Thus the 'devil's advocate' has been summoned from the devil to present his argument. His opponent in the discussions is known as the *advocatus dei* ('God's advocate'), who presents the case in favour of beatification or canonization.

To be **Entering the Lion's Den** is to be facing a hostile situation, which will undoubtedly test your character and nerve before an outcome is decided. The modern use of the phrase implies that such a task is undertaken voluntarily but not without caution. However, back in the days when the Romans had such fun throwing humans into a pit full of hungry lions to be torn to shreds in the name of entertainment, the idea had an entirely different sense, as thieves and murderers would be executed in this way (plus the odd Christian for good measure). The Old Testament (Daniel 6:16) describes a similar occasion when King Darius was persuaded to sentence one of his most senior ministers to death for publicly praying to his own god, instead of the king's – a serious matter in such enlightened times: 'So at last the king gave the order for Daniel's arrest and he was taken to the den of lions. The king said to him, "May your God, whom you worship continually, deliver you", and then they threw him in.' God did indeed 'deliver' Daniel, who emerged from the lions' den the next day without so much as a scratch on him. The lions didn't come off too badly either as the officials who betrayed Daniel were thrown into the den instead (plus all the other members of their families, to round off the feast).

To **Learn and Inwardly Digest** is a phrase we use to suggest contemplation of a subject in order to learn from it. The source of this expression is found in a prayer for the second Sunday of Advent, in *The Book of Common Prayer*: 'Grant that we may in such wise hear them, read, mark, learn and inwardly digest them.'

To **Pour Oil on Troubled Waters** is to calm down a heated situation or to prevent an argument or a dispute from raging out of control. The root of this expression can be found in a legend recalled by the Venerable Bede in his *Ecclesiastical History of the English People* (731). The story tells of a priest named Utta who was given the job of escorting King Oswy's bride across the sea. The weather looked troublesome and Utta was not keen on the task until approached by Bishop Aiden, who gave him a bottle of holy oil. The bishop had foreseen a storm at sea but reassured Utta that the oil would immediately calm the waters and make his journey safe and comfortable. As expected, a fierce storm did descend upon the boat, terrifying the king's bride and leaving all the sailors fearing for their lives. That is, of course, until Utta remembered the bishop's words, found the bottle and poured the oil over the side. The sea was immediately calmed and everybody completed the voyage in safety. Since then, it has been the 'oil' of soothing language or actions that have calmed troubled waters of a figurative kind. Obviously I cannot confirm if this story is true or not, but it is certainly where we find the source of one of our favourite expressions.

If someone announces they are **Washing Their Hands of Something**, they are declaring they no longer wish to be involved in the matter and will therefore not be implicated in the outcome of events. The suggestion is that things are bound to go wrong and dissociation is the best course of action. The origin of the phrase can be found in the Bible. In the passage describing the trial of Jesus (Matthew 27:24), Pontius Pilate, who was in charge of sentencing him, declares to the masses that Jesus is innocent 'as far as he could tell', but the crowd bay for blood and demand an execution. When Pilate realizes his appeal is accomplishing nothing, apart from inciting the people to riot, he takes a bowl of water and announces: 'I am innocent of the blood of this righteous man. You see to it.' Which, as history shows us, is just what they did.

PEOPLE AND PLACES

The Streets Are Paved with Gold is an indication that a particular town or city is full of opportunity and well worth a visit. George Colman the Younger wrote, in *The Heir-at-Law* (1797): 'Oh, London is a fine town, a very famous city, where all the streets are paved with gold, and all the maidens pretty.' (Having now researched this claim extensively over the last 20 years, I can assure the reader that the younger George is only half right.) But Colman did not coin the expression, which can be found in a popular legend that tells the story of Dick Whittington, who as a 13-year-old boy packed his worldly goods into his handkerchief, tied it on the end of a stick and made his way from Gloucestershire to London after hearing the pavements there were made of gold and silver. There is no record of the story being told before 1605 but there *was* a real Dick

Whittington who was born in the village of Pauntly in Gloucestershire and who was actually Lord Mayor of London four times between the late 1300s and early 1400s. He was also 13 years old when he left home. There is a suggestion that the expression began to be used after the Goldsmiths' Company merged with the Paviours' Company and hence the connection. However, going back even further in time, we have yet another reference, and probably the original one. The Book of Revelation (21:21) insists that the streets of heaven are paved with gold –'the streets of the city were pure gold'.

To be **Blessed with the Gift of Blarney** means a person is able to talk their way into another's affections, or indeed out of trouble, with considerable ease. This expression can be traced to Ireland and an historic event that took place in 1602. During the reign of Elizabeth I, the English army besieged Blarney Castle in southern Ireland and the owner, Dermot Macarthy, and his soldiers found themselves trapped inside. Dermot, also known as Cormac Macarthy, was ordered to surrender his property as a show of loyalty to the queen, but he had no intention of doing that. He also had no intention of starving to death, so adopted gentle diplomacy as an answer to his problem. After many excuses and much prevarication, which included plenty of flattering letters and messages to the queen, the siege eventually failed when Elizabeth finally gave in to his Irish charm. However, at one point she had become so frustrated with Macarthy's delaying tactics she famously exclaimed: 'Odds bodkins, that's more Blarney talk.' These days the legend is that if a visitor should place a kiss on a particular stone at Blarney Castle, they too will be blessed with Macarthy's gift of the gab.

A **Smart Aleck** is someone just too clever for their own good. It has been recorded that the most likely origin for this expression is the New York City con man and fraudster Aleck Hoag. During the 1840s, the scoundrel had his wife posing as a prostitute and between them they would rob their customers, knowing few men would report the crime to the police under such compromising circumstances. However, on some occasions the pair were caught, although Hoag managed to escape prosecution by bribing the officers involved. But then Hoag tried to be a little too clever by cutting the arresting policeman out of the deal, convinced this would be overlooked should previous police corruption become apparent during any prosecution, but he was wrong and found himself in jail. Policemen in New York from then onwards used the expression 'smart aleck' to describe anybody pushing their luck too far.

To **Go Like Billio** means to be operating at full speed, and with gusto too. There are several explanations for this expression, which began to be used widely during the 19th century. First we find a reference to Nino Biglio, who was a lieutenant under Garibaldi. He would race into battle and fight fearlessly; hence the phrase 'to fight like Biglio' was regularly used at the time. The second possibility lies with Stephenson's first-ever steam engine, known as 'Puffing Billy', which some believe is the root of the expression, but I prefer the final explanation. Joseph Billio was an especially zealous Puritan preacher who founded the Independent Congregation at Maldon in Essex in 1682. Billio was famous for his wild, ranting sermons and seems to have inspired the phrase. It passed into popular use thanks to P. G. Wodehouse, who wrote, in *The Code of the Woosters* (1938):

> 'But, Bertie, this sounds as if you were not going to sit in.'
> 'It was how I meant it to sound.'
> 'You wouldn't fail me, would you?'
> 'I would. I would fail you like Billio.'

To **Close Your Eyes and Think of England** is advice given to a person on how to tolerate an unwanted and unpleasant activity, usually sexual in nature. But it is offered as humorous guidance rather than as a serious suggestion. This phrase has been in regular use since 1912 when the journal of Lady Hillingdon was published, which included the lines: 'I am happy now that Charles calls on my bedchamber less frequently than of old. As it is, I now endure but two calls a week and when I hear his steps outside my door I lie down on my bed, close my eyes, open my legs and think of England.' Good to see romance was still alive and well back then.

Not so much a phrase, but a word that is worth tracing, **Tarmac** is the smooth black surface we lay on roads, paths and playgrounds all over Britain. It was designed in 1815 by a Scottish engineer called John Loudon McAdam (1756–1836), after whom the new substance was named. During experiments to construct a cheap, durable road surface, McAdam developed a material of crushed stone and gravel bound together with a layer of tar which was both strong, flexible and allowed water to drain away. The material is in fact called tarmacadam, but this has been shortened over time and is now only ever known by its nickname, 'tarmac'.

'**Before You Can Say Jack Robinson** it'll all be over.' How many times have we heard someone say something like this and wondered who Jack Robinson was? To trace Jack we have to go back over two hundred years to 1778 when Fanny Burney first used the expression in her novel *Evelina*. In the text, Fanny indicates the phrase is already well known in the way she regularly uses it to describe something that happens 'in an instant'. There are also suggestions that Jack Robinson was featured shortly afterwards in a play. But let's now turn to an exchange that took place in the House of Commons in the late 1700s and was famously reported across all Europe, thanks to the drama and contentiousness of the occasion.

It is worth recording that back then, and for that matter now, members of the House would refrain from mentioning any other member by name, a practice that came about in avoidance of the strict libel laws of the time. Instead, an MP might suggest that 'the Honourable Member for Shaggy Dog constituency has today shown himself to be a scoundrel by stating that ... ', thereby avoiding mentioning the person's name but making it quite clear whom they were referring to. We can still hear this mode of address today in Parliament, but these days it is merely due to tradition, rather than the avoidance of libel. You can imagine, then, how much of a fuss was caused in the late 18th century by playwright and MP Richard Brinsley Sheridan when he was asked in the House to name a member of government under suspicion and accused of bribery. Without hesitation, Sheridan looked across at fellow MP John Robinson and announced, 'I could name him for you as soon as I could say Jack Robinson.' Well, that remark was a little too close for comfort, even by today's standards, causing uproar and being reported across the land. It is likely this exchange led to the use of the phrase by Fanny Burney in her popular novel and hence its passage into the English language, but I have found an even earlier source for the term and quite possibly for Sheridan's use of it.

A poem by Thomas Hudson, entitled 'Jack Robinson' and written in the early 17th century, told the tale of a sailor returning from the high seas to find the love of his life already married to another. The sad sonnet includes the line 'and so he went back to sea, afore you could say Jack Robinson'. It is quite likely that Sheridan, literary fellow that he was, knew this poem and was deliberately quoting from it to avoid censure in the House. By substituting the name of John Robinson, the MP he accused, with the name of the fictional character in Hudson's poem, he could claim the similarity between the two names as merely coincidental should Robinson ever be vindicated and threaten libel action. Clever stuff: no wonder the exchange was so widely reported and admired.

'**Gordon Bennett!**' is a remark we have probably all used at one time or another to express surprise and even respect. James Gordon Bennett II was born in America in 1841, the son of Gordon Bennett, the founder of the *New York Herald*. With cash to spare, he lived a charmed life and when he eventually inherited his father's newspaper empire, began a spending spree estimated at US$40 million (the total sum spent between 1881 and 1918). Gordon Bennett junior was a flamboyant character who enjoyed encouraging the innovative and exciting, such as the first-ever aeroplane race, the Gordon Bennett Cup, which was won by Glenn Curtis in 1909. He sponsored a balloon race in France known as the Coupe Aéronautique Gordon Bennett, as well as yacht races, boxing championships, steam engine trials and car races. It was Gordon Bennett who funded Henry Morton Stanley's expedition to Africa in search of the missionary Dr Livingstone and also financed the ill-fated Jeannette expedition to the Arctic.

For his own part, Bennett was an extraordinary character who once flew a plane through an open barn as a stunt, burned a bulky roll of cash, which was in his back pocket causing discomfort, and urinated in his future in-laws' fireplace, in front of other guests, after drunkenly mistaking it for a toilet. He also regularly annoyed fellow diners in top restaurants with his habit of pulling all the tablecloths away, sending food and crockery crashing. Unsurprisingly, he was once horsewhipped on the steps of a gentlemen's club and eventually forced to flee in 1887 when he turned up in Paris and continued to run his newspaper empire from there. Despite some outrageous behaviour, Bennett was essentially a benevolent and visionary man who gave large amounts to charity and founded the Associated Press news service, which exists today, as does Bennett's newspaper, in the shape of the *International Herald Tribune*. In his lifetime, Bennett's newspapers would regularly run the headline 'Gordon Bennett' while reporting his antics, and his name thus became associated with anything outrageous, exciting and over the top.

It is also worth recording the story of another Gordon Bennett, a prolific although barely known biscuit maker, born in 1878. Some people believe the phrase entered the language after 'Biscuit Bennett' (as he was known) used to cycle the streets of Pontefract calling out his own name to advertise his product.

When a person finally **Meets His Waterloo** it means he (or she) has suffered a comprehensive defeat after enjoying a run of great success. By 1815, Napoleon Bonaparte had created an empire that incorporated nearly all of Europe. His battlefield successes between 1809 and 1811 had been complete and his military strategy was feared and respected across the continent, until, that is, 18 June 1815, and the events that took place near the small town of Waterloo in Belgium. It was here that the Duke of Wellington and his allied forces, despite being heavily outnumbered, finally crushed Napoleon's army, sending the Frenchman spiralling into exile and captivity on the island of St Helena, where he died in 1821. The Battle of Waterloo ended 26 years of war between the major European powers and France (the Napoleonic Wars) and peace finally fell across the continent once again. The idiom 'to meet your Waterloo' has thus been in use for nearly two hundred years and is a clear reference to the former French emperor. The Duke of

Wellington, on the other hand, has had to make do with a simple waterproof boot favoured by gardeners – although to be fair he has since been honoured via a coat, a bomber aircraft, a chest of drawers, a card game, a public school, a coniferous tree (the wellingtonia), an apple, a hat and a pair of trousers.

There is a charming footnote to this story. In 1802, Napoleon was the first person to declare an interest in building a tunnel beneath the English Channel, joining Britain and France. Cartoons at the time showed French troops travelling under the sea via the tunnel. When it finally was built in the 1990s, some French bureaucrats suggested it should be called the Napoleon Line after the French hero, but the idea was later dropped. That is a shame, because where does the railway link end on this side of the Channel? At Waterloo (station) of course.

King Louis XVI and Queen Marie Antoinette ruled France until 1792 when the French Revolution cut their reign short. As it turned out, the **Guillotine** (see entry) also cut them a little shorter themselves during the period of the Revolution known as 'La Terreur'. But the French royal family weren't always so unpopular with their subjects. On 6 October 1789, starving men and women made a pilgrimage to the Palace of Versailles where the royal family greeted them personally and handed out freshly baked bread to the needy. This earned the king the affectionate nickname of '**The Baker**' and Marie

Antoinette became known as 'The Baker's Wife'. In turn their son, the Dauphin, came to be called 'the Shop Boy'. Bread has long been associated with many historical events, but rarely considered actually responsible for them, as many believe in the case of the French Revolution.

During the late 1780s, the price of bread was soaring throughout France and the peasants were, quite literally, revolting. In August 1788, roughly half of an urban worker's (or peasant's) income was spent on bread. But by July the following year, that figure had risen to 80 per cent. It was then that Marie Antoinette was supposed to have said, on being informed of the great bread shortage throughout the land: 'Well, let them eat cake instead.' It is generally accepted that the French queen never actually made such a remark, but it is a good indication of the mood of the nation that those in opposition to the aristocracy were able to use such propaganda to suggest just how out of touch the king and queen were with their people. On 14 July 1789, only a few days after this remark was reported, hundreds of Parisian women stormed the Bastille prison. The fall of the Bastille marked the start of the French Revolution and from that point there was no turning back – all for the lack of bread.

The word **Bedlam** is used to describe a place of uncontrollable confusion and uproar. In 1247, the Priory of St Mary of Bethlehem was established in

London and 300 years later, in 1547, the building was given to the city by Henry VIII as a hospital called Bethlem, used to house the mentally unstable and insane. Later still, the asylum was transferred to Moorfields (which is now the Imperial War Museum) and, once it had become established there, became a popular tourist attraction. Incredibly, the governors charged admission for tickets, enabling the public to witness the bizarre behaviour of the inmates, and in many cases even encouraged visitors to goad them on. The asylum became known as 'Bedlam' and the word associated with human degradation and the public's inhumane indifference to it. (Which is a little alarming because as a small boy my bedroom used to be called 'bedlam', and it's much worse in there today.) In 1800, it moved again to Lambeth and again in 1930 to Aldington in Surrey. Today it is known as the Bethlehem Royal Hospital and located in Beckenham in Kent.

To **Bone Up** on something is to study intensively and gain as much information about a matter as possible. It was originally thought that this expression indicated adding to a person's knowledge in the same way that adding more bone, or 'boning up', would help stiffen a whalebone corset. But there is strong evidence to suggest the expression in fact derives from the translator and bibliographer Henry Bohn (1796–1884), who made his name as a second-hand bookseller and publisher of cheap editions and whose libraries served both students and the wider public. When his translations of the Classics were published, they became literary handbooks for students who were studying or 'cramming' ('Bohning up') for an examination.

Bob's Your Uncle is used to describe something that is resolved in your favour without much effort, as in: 'Just send the form in and Bob's your uncle.' The phrase was in regular use in England from the 1890s after the promotion in 1886 of Arthur Balfour to Secretary of State for Ireland. Balfour was a surprise choice for the position and few regarded him as qualified for the post. But when it became known he was the nephew of British prime minister Robert Gascoyne-Cecil, 3rd Marquis of Salisbury, the joke circulated that if Robert was your uncle, then anything was possible.

A **Calamity Jane** is an affectionate name for a young girl who gets herself into all sorts of trouble without really meaning to. The original Calamity Jane was Martha Jane Canary (1852–1903) of Deadwood in South Dakota, USA. She notoriously behaved like a cowboy and was, unsurprisingly, unlucky in love. Or at least her husbands were unlucky in love as 11 out of the 12 of them died in suspicious circumstances. Calamity Jane dressed, swore, rode, drank and fought like a man. She also famously threatened 'calamity' to any man who offended her in the smallest of ways. It sounds like she must have been reincarnated and then I made the mistake of almost marrying her in the 1990s. (See also **Bunny Boiler**.)

Dr Livingstone, I Presume? is an expression that has been used for over a hundred years to express comic surprise when chancing upon old friends in unexpected places. Dr David Livingstone (1813–73) was a Scottish missionary and explorer. Once, after a long period of travelling in central Africa, he became cut off from the outside world and not a word was heard from him for many years. It is said that American newspaper owner **Gordon Bennett** (see entry) paid for the American journalist Henry Morton Stanley to look for him, expecting the event to make headline news. The 27-year-old correspondent set off in 1869 and found the missionary two years later at Lake Tanganyika. It was there he uttered the now famous phrase 'Dr Livingstone, I presume?' The remark not only made headline news at the time, but is still being talked about to this day.

In America, a **John Hancock** is a term for signing an autograph. John Hancock was a prominent Boston merchant whose signature, as president of the Continental Congress, appears as one of the first on the American Declaration of Independence of 1776. The signature is also by far the largest, and legend has it that Hancock, while adding his name to the document, commented: 'There – I guess King

George or John Bull will be able to read that without his spectacles.' The phrase became common parlance at the turn of the 19th/20th century.

A **Jack the Lad** is known to be carefree, bold and perhaps a little troublesome at times, although generally popular with his peers. The original 'lad' was Jack Sheppard, the 22-year-old son of an English carpenter born in London's Spitalfields area in 1702. His criminal antics made him notorious throughout England and he eventually became the subject of numerous plays and popular ballads of the time. He was repeatedly arrested and even imprisoned on four occasions and each time managed to effect a spectacular escape despite once being manacled to the floor and in solitary confinement. He escaped from St Giles's prison by sawing through the wooden ceiling and making his way across the roof tops of nearby houses, and he managed to pick the locks of his manacles using only his finger nail, then climbed a chimney to freedom. Such daring deeds captured the public imagination and he became something of a hero among ruffians. Apparently on the fifth attempt to escape, he was captured by Jonathan Wilde (see **Double Cross**) and, despite a further escape attempt, was finally hanged on the gallows at Tyburn in front of a crowd of reputedly 200,000 people. His body now lies in the churchyard of St Martin in the Fields.

*

A **Maverick** is an unorthodox individual who is independent minded and often quite innovative. Samuel A. Maverick (1803–70) was a cattle rancher in Texas who was well known throughout the state for leaving his cattle unbranded, which was something no other rancher had dared to do for fear of rustlers. Maverick not only regarded the practice of branding cruel to his animals, but he also realized that he himself could then claim any unbranded animals as his own, as everybody would agree that they must be his. Maverick was so well known that, by the time of his death, his name was being used to describe politicians who refused to affiliate themselves with a particular cause, and the expression has widened in its application ever since.

To **Mesmerize** a person, or even a crowd of people, is to leave them spellbound at what they have seen, as if in a trance. Dr Franz Anton Mesmer (1734–1815) was a leading Austrian physician who pioneered the use of hypnotism as a way of treating illness. He practised in Vienna and believed that good health was the result of a harmonious ebb and flow of magnetic fluid circulating the body and that disease and illness were caused by a blockage in this flow pattern. After inducing a patient into a trance-like state, Mesmer would pass a magnet over the person's body in an attempt to free the flow and thereby cure the illness. This marked the birth of hypnotism and it also opened the door to attempts at paranormal communication, which soon gathered pace throughout the world. The medical profession discredited Mesmer's theory of 'animal magnetism' during his lifetime, although a pupil managed to re-establish his reputation after his death, referring to his theories as **Mesmerism**. The term was current by 1829 and the associated word, 'mesmerized', used to describe someone in a trance-like state.

To call a person a **Right Proper Charlie** is rhyming slang upon rhyming slang, and you may never wish to use this apparently inoffensive remark ever again. We know that a **Right Charlie** is simply a harmless fool, the full phrase starting out as a 'Charlie Smirke', rhyming slang for 'berk', the name of a successful English jockey who raced between the 1930s and 1950s. To call somebody a **Berk** is also generally regarded as an affectionate and humorous put-down, lacking any malice, but the origin of the phrase suggests it is entirely offensive, or at least was to begin with. 'Berk' derives from another piece of cockney rhyming slang in which someone referred to as a 'Berkshire hunt' would be on the receiving end of one of the most offensive swearwords in the English language. 'Berkshire hunt' was then shortened to 'berk'. These days, however, 'berk' or 'right Charlie' are not regarded as particularly unpleasant by anybody and not at all linked to the original meaning by those using it – so don't get on your **High Horse** (see entry)!

Sadomasochism is the term made up of two slightly connected words used to describe anybody who is partial either to inflicting pain on another person or having pain inflicted upon themselves. **Sadist** is the word we use to describe anybody who obtains gratification through the infliction of humiliation or pain on another person or animal. It – **Sadism**, that is – is the morbid physiological state of actually enjoying cruelty. The term derives from the author Marquis de Sade (1740–1814), whose works of sexual perversion include *Justine* (1791), *La Philosophie dans le boudoir* (1793) and *Les Crimes de l'amour* (1800). Naturally, given the century he lived in, his work raised a few eyebrows, among other things. While some regarded him as depraved and dangerous, others considered him years ahead of his time. He is, without doubt, the most infamous writer in French literary history. Let us now turn to Leopold von Sacher-Masoch (1835–1895), an

Austrian novelist who experimented, both personally and through his writings, with the inflicting of
severe pain upon himself by women. The polar
opposite to the Marquis de Sade, Sacher-Masoch
would receive gratification by being tortured and
humiliated. Unsurprisingly, he ended his life in an
asylum and the only surprising thing is that he managed to live for so long. As it was, he lived out his
remaining days happily receiving electric shock treatment administered by large Hungarian nurses with
bushy moustaches and burly forearms. It was a
German psychiatrist Krafft-Ebing (1840–1902) who
coined the term **Masochism** to describe the condition, which has attracted enthusiastic devotees ever
since. The combined practice of both de Sade and
Sacher-Masoch has since been labelled 'sadomasochism'.

I have a friend whose partner, a few years ago,
continuously tried persuading her to join him in
such activities. That was until one day, when he was
being particularly persistent; she took aim and
volleyed him straight in the **Goolies** (see entry).
Apparently he went down like a shot elephant,
whereupon she bent over him and asked very sweetly,
'Is that painful enough for you darling?' then packed
her bags.

A **Silly Billy** is a phrase we affectionately use to
describe a person, usually a child, who has got up
to some kind of mischief. It can also be applied to

an adult, usually male, who has been involved in some daft misbehaviour and now has to face the consequences of his actions. The original Billy was King George III's uncle William Frederick, the Duke of Gloucester (1776–1834), who was known to be of weak intellect and managed to get up to all sorts of embarrassing and stupid antics at court. The word 'silly' derives from the Old English word *soelig*, meaning 'happy' or 'blessed', and during the Middle Ages it was pronounced 'seely' in many English dialects. By then, the word had changed to mean feeble, unsophisticated and ignorant.

When we **Turn a Blind Eye** it suggests we know what is going on and what is about to happen, but fail to take any action to alter the situation. It is a phrase emanating from one of the most significant events in British naval history. During the Battle of Copenhagen, in 1801, the commander of the British fleet, Admiral Sir Hyde Parker, watched as Horatio Nelson launched an attack on the Danish navy. At one point, Parker felt that the fleet was taking unnecessary risks and bearing unacceptable losses, so he ordered Nelson, via a series of flags, to disengage with the enemy. But when Nelson's officers pointed out the order, he famously raised a telescope to his blind eye and replied: 'Order, what order? I see no ships.' Nelson then returned his attention to the battle and soundly defeated the Danes. On his return to London, he was made a viscount and put in overall command of the Channel fleet, which led to his defining moment at the Battle of Trafalgar in 1805.

To present something **Warts and All** is to make no attempt to cover any defects or hide unsightly detail. It has always been customary for portrait painters to soften the features of their subjects by removing blemishes and facial lines from their work to improve upon nature. But when Oliver Cromwell, as Lord Protector of England in the mid 17th century, commissioned Sir Peter Lely to paint his portrait, he issued the artist with the following instructions: 'I desire you would use all your skill to paint my picture truly like I am and not flatter me at all. Remark all these roughness, pimples, warts and everything as you see me, otherwise I will never pay you a farthing for it.' The end result does indeed include a large wart just below Cromwell's lower lip.

ANIMALISTIC

If we describe a person as **Stuck Up** it is safe to assume they are a little aloof and behaving in a superior manner. The expression recalls the way peacocks habitually 'stick up' their tail feathers as if to display their importance or superiority over fellow peacocks.

The **Booby Prize** is the prize given to a person or team who comes last in an event. A 'booby' is in fact a slow-witted South American bird that is easy to catch. In the 17th century, sailors found that a simple noose set on deck with a few dried biscuits as bait was enough to trap the daft bird – hence the phrase **Booby Trap**. As an extension of this, slow-witted sailors were known as 'boobies' and consequently the prize for being in last place in a contest had to be a 'booby prize'. This expression passed from the high seas into wider use via the whist drives that were all the rage at the time. The prize for coming last at such an event was traditionally the booby prize and this term has since been applied to almost any kind of competition imaginable.

To be **As Bald as a Badger** or **As Bald as a Coot** are phrases used regularly in both America and Britain respectively, the latter having been in use since around 1430. The aquatic coot is often known as the 'bald coot' because the white flash on the bird's head is thought to resemble a man's bald pate. The badger simile, on the other hand, has been shortened over time and in fact started life as 'bald as a badger's bum'. The reason for this is that for centuries the bristles on a gentleman's shaving brush were made out of luxurious badger's hair, plucked from the poor creature's backside. In fact, top-of-the-range shaving brushes are still made out of badger's hair to this day (or at least they are claimed to be). Obviously the little fellow would not need to be killed for this and, given that hair could re-grow and then be plucked again, it would seem that thousands of the red-faced creatures would be left to roam the countryside with a bald backside, until the next shaving-brush-plucking season came around (if there was such a thing). I know not whether the badger in question would need to be male or female, or if that matters anyway, but the main question is this: who got the job of plucking it? Or was it even a two-man job? In which case, who did the holding and who did the plucking? I'm off to try and find out right now.

A **Stool Pigeon** is an informer or a police spy. This is a hunting expression and reveals the common practice of tying (sometimes even nailing) a pigeon to a high stool as a decoy for other pigeons, which would then land nearby and be at the mercy of waiting hunters. The expression was in regular use by 1825.

To be the **Bee's Knees** is to be regarded as the best, superior to everyone (or everything) else. Some people insist this phrase actually has something to do with those little knees. Once a bee has flown into a flower, pollen sticks to its body and the insect then carefully transfers it to sacs on its rear legs. Authorities in the apian world maintain that the term stems from the delicate way in which bees bend those diminutive leg joints to perform this task. I don't know about that, but I do know the phrase was widely used in the 1700s as 'as big as a bee's knee', while in the 1800s it had changed to 'as weak as a bee's knee'.

During the 1920s, it became popular in America to use a London-style rhyming slang, picked up by soldiers mixing with their English counterparts during the First World War. By the time they had settled back in the States, imaginative Americans were making up their own version, which was soon popularized via films, songs and stories. Some examples used at the time, and always taken to mean the best of everything, were: the cat's pyjamas, the cat's cufflinks, the clam's garter, the tiger's stripes, the leopard's spots, the pig's wings, the snake's hips, the eel's ankle, the cat's whiskers, the mutt's nuts (later expanded to a slightly ruder version) and the bee's knees. These last three are the only ones to have survived and remain in regular use – all meaning the same thing.

Our unusual fascination with bees has spawned an array of idioms that we all take for granted: **As Busy as a Bee**, meaning to work hard at something, **Making a Beeline** (see also **As the Crow Flies**), meaning to go directly for something (in America they use the word 'airline' in exactly the same way). The phrase derives from the ancient belief that a bee always flew in a straight line from its nectar gathering to the hive, although that piece of folklore has since been proved to be untrue. A **Bee in Your Bonnet** describes the manner of someone who is flapping around and making a fuss, as you might if there were actually a bee in your hat. The **Queen Bee** is the lady who believes herself to be, or is believed to be, in charge of everyone else. The Greek philosopher Plato was known as the **Athenian Bee**, so called because of the legend that, as a baby, a swarm of bees settled on his mouth when he was still in his cradle, so that all his words flowed with the sweetness of honey. Meanwhile Sophocles, the Greek tragic poet, was known as the **Attic Bee** due to the sweetness of his sonnets and, as some believe, the place in his house where he wrote them, although 'Attic' in this instance means 'relating to ancient Athens', which is where both Sophocles and Plato hailed from.

To **Bear Up** means to keep your spirits high and remain cheerful when things aren't going well. It is a determined show of self-confidence in the face of adversity. There are two possible origins. The first can be found in nautical language where the term 'bear up' means to steer a sailing ship more closely into the wind, which is more challenging than steering away from the wind (or 'bearing off'). A second, and more likely possibility, derives from the carriage horses that were used in the days before motorized transport. The 'bearing rein' was part of the harness used to hold a horse's neck in a proud, upright position during ceremonies. When, at the end of a long exhausting parade, a horse began to show signs of fatigue, the bearing rein was used to pull its head back into position and the poor animal was known to be 'bearing upwards'.

A **Toady** is a sycophant, a person who will do anything to earn a superior's respect and affection. During the Middle Ages, quack doctors, or charlatans, would employ an impoverished person (usually a starving man who would do absolutely anything to earn a crust) to work with them while they tried to sell their remedies. Typically, the unfortunate person would consume an apparently poisonous toad, in front of a gathering, so that the doctor could then prove his remedies would cure the contaminated man. Naturally, the toad was not poisonous in the first place. If it had been, then the man would have died as the quack's remedies never worked anyway, but the doctor's 'toady' was still prepared to eat in public a live creature, and a disgusting one at that, for the sake of a loaf of bread.

A **Shaggy Dog Story** is a story of unconvincing origin, not necessarily to be believed. The origin of this phrase is, in fact, a real shaggy dog story, dating from the 1800s. Apparently a wealthy gentleman, who owned a grand residence in Park Lane, lost his beloved shaggy dog during a walk across Hyde Park, opposite his home. The man was heartbroken and advertised extensively in *The Times* for the return of his valuable companion. Meanwhile, an American living in New York had heard the news and taken great pity on the dog's owner. He vowed he would search for a pet matching the description of the lost hound and deliver it to London on his next business visit, which he duly did. But when the New Yorker presented himself at the palatial London mansion, he was met by a po-faced butler who, the story goes, looked down at the dog, bowed, winced and then exclaimed: 'But not as shaggy as that, sir!' The story provoked howls of laughter among London socialites, but was not entirely believed by everybody. A shaggy dog story indeed.

A Little Bird Told Me is a phrase we use when we do not want to reveal the source of our information, but most people could be expected to guess correctly anyway. It is an expression we have used since the mid 16th century and is thought to have its root in a charming little story from the Book of Kings in the Bible about a meeting between the Queen of Sheba and King Solomon, which goes something like this. Once upon a time all the birds in the land were summoned to appear before the great King Solomon, which they duly did. Well, all apart from a small lapwing whose absence could not be explained by any of the other birds. When the lapwing finally appeared,

she was questioned about her absence and explained she had been to visit the Queen of Sheba and that the queen was making preparations to visit King Solomon. The king was pleased with the news and began to make preparations at court to receive his guest. Meanwhile, the little bird flew off to Ethiopia and told the queen that the king had a great desire to meet her and so she excitedly began making plans for the trip. The famed meeting thus took place thanks to the lapwing. When King Solomon asked the Queen of Sheba how the visit had been arranged, she replied: 'A little bird told me.' The King, of course, had to admit that 'a little bird' had told him too. And this is a true story! Oh, all right then, it isn't – but it is a good one. For the real truth we have to go, once again, to the Bible and the Book of Ecclesiastes (10:20): 'Curse not the king, no not in your thoughts. And curse not the rich in your bedchamber either for a little bird of the air shall carry the voice, and that which has wings shall tell the matter.' Whatever all that means!

To have **Bats in the Belfry** is a wonderfully English way of describing the harmlessly insane, eccentric or mentally challenged. To call a person **Bats** or **Batty** is a natural extension of this. The allusion is to bats flapping around in the bell tower of a church or cathedral in a wild and frenzied manner once the ringing has woken them up. But how has this expression come about?

There are suggestions that the phrase is rooted

in the medical profession, and in particular William Battie MD (1704–76), an early psychiatrist and the esteemed author of *A Treatise on Madness* (1758). The phrase is also linked to an eminent barrister from Spanish Town, Jamaica, by the name of Robert Fitzherbert Batty, who travelled to England in the early 1800s. Fitzherbert Batty was so well known in London that when he was certified insane in 1839 it made big news, which also soon travelled back to the West Indies. It would be nice to connect either of these characters to the source of the expression, but in fact there is no real evidence of the phrase being used prior to 1900.It is possible one of them could be the source of the expression, but I wouldn't want to guarantee it. We do know for sure, however, that a play entitled *Bats in the Belfry*, written by Diana Morgan and Robert MacDermot, was produced at Golders Green Hippodrome in North End Road, Barnet, from 16 August 1937 and that the cast included a young Charles Hawtrey of *Carry On* fame.

Finally, there is evidence of the term being used, in print at least, by the critic Stephen Graham, who wrote in *London Nights* in 1925: 'There is a set of jokes which are the common property of many comedians. You can hear them just as easily in Leicester

Square as you can in Mile End Road. It strikes the unwonted visitor to the Pavilion as very original when Stanley Lupino says of someone, "He has bats in the belfry", as it is not always understood that the expression belongs to the music hall at large.'

A Cat Has Nine Lives is a proverb dating back to around 1546. The belief is that cats are naturally able to land safely upon their feet from whatever height they are dropped and this gives them an obvious ability to get out of all sorts of trouble. (Not so fast, kids – bring that cat back downstairs immediately!) In ancient Egypt, as in many parts of the world, cats had the reputation of being the perfect rat catchers and were an important means of ridding a city of the plague-spreading vermin. In Egypt, cats were also regarded as sacred, associated with the trinity of mother, father and son, and it was believed that if you multiplied the sacred number of three by three, you had calculated the number of lives the revered cat actually had. Which some would say makes them perfect to experiment on.

To **Foul Your Own Nest** is to spoil what you have established (in particular close relationships in family and business) and prejudice your interests in the process. This expression is actually an old proverb, known for over a thousand years, that warns: 'It is a foul bird that defiles its own nest.' The moral of the saying derives from the observation that a bird will not excrete in its own nest and will also clean up the waste of its young. Any of us who have to park our cars under trees during the months of spring will have known that already.

To **Get into a Scrape** is to find yourself in an awkward and embarrassing situation as a result of your own carelessness. There is a story dating back to the early 1800s that may well prove to be the origin of this expression. 'Scrapes' are holes in the earth that a deer will habitually dig by using its forefeet. They can be up to 45 cm deep and anybody, either on foot or on horseback, might easily find themselves 'in a scrape', which could result in injury. On one such occasion, in 1803, it is said that Mrs Frances Tucker, who lived in Devon, was walking in Powderham Park and slipped into a scrape. A furious stag then charged and killed the unfortunate lady.

Not to Have a Cat in Hell's Chance is an unusual expression, to say the least, one that has been in use since the 1600s. To understand how it may have entered the language, we need to reveal the full phrase, which is: 'No more chance than a cat in hell would have without claws' – first recorded in Francis Grose's *Classical Dictionary of the Vulgar Tongue* (1796). Well, that clears that one up then.

To be **Having Kittens** is an expression used to describe an hysterically nervous person, who is petrified about a forthcoming event. The expression was used in America from around 1900 before being taken up in Britain. During the Middle Ages, doctors apparently believed that if a pregnant woman was experiencing pains then she must be 'bewitched' and had a litter of kittens inside her womb that were clawing at her. Witches, it was said, could provide the potions that would destroy the imagined kittens. Incredibly, as late as the 17th century the legal term for 'obtaining an abortion' was still presented in the law courts as 'removing cats in the belly'.

To **Keep the Wolf from the Door** is to find a way of warding off poverty, and hunger in particular. Since ancient times, the wolf has been a symbol of starvation and destitution, and almost all fables and legends depict the wolf as desperate and ravenous, as Little Red Riding Hood would testify to if asked. The French have a saying, '*manger comme un loup*', meaning 'to eat like a wolf', and the Germans have a similar expression: *Wolfshunger*. In England and other parts of Europe, 'keeping the wolf from the door', meaning 'to ward off starvation', has been in use since the 15th century.

THE WORKING DAY

The Tower of London is traditionally guarded by Yeoman Warders, who have been called **Beefeaters** since the latter half of the 15th century. Formed in 1485 as the royal bodyguard at Henry VII's coronation, they were also known as the Yeomen of the Guard. Henry VIII appointed them as warders at the Tower of London, called the Yeomen Extraordinary of the Guard, during the early 16th century, and we know that around that time servants were called 'eaters', with those of a slightly higher rank labelled 'loafeaters'. In keeping with their elevated status, the Yeoman Warders became known at the Tower as 'Beefeaters', reflecting the generous meat rations they were given.

On **Bank Holidays** most employees, apart from those in the service sector, are given the day off. Today these are officially known as 'public holidays', but the original expression is still in general use across the world. It all started at the Bank of England in the 19th century. Until 1830, the world's premier bank was closed for more than 40 days in every 12 months. But during that year the number was dropped to 18 and only four years later reduced again to just four. Since then there have been some slight adjustments but for many years now we appear to have settled upon eight. They are: New Year's Day, Good Friday, Easter Monday, May Day, the spring and August bank holidays, Christmas Day and Boxing Day.

For students of finer detail, I have looked into the origin of the name we give **Boxing Day**. The day following Christmas Day was formerly known as St Stephen's Day. For centuries it was customary for religious folk to leave a box in church, during the Christmas Mass, which was packed full of gifts and money. The contents, known as 'the dole of the Christmas box' or 'the box money', would then be distributed by priests to the needy on the following day (St Stephen's Day), which subsequently became known as 'the box day'. It was also customary for young apprentices and boys to carry a box around on St Stephen's Day to their masters' clients in order to receive small gratuities. These 'Christmas tips' would be placed in the box and shared among all the apprentices. Prior to this, the custom was known as 'Handsel Day' (from the Old English word *handselen*, meaning quite literally 'to deliver into the hand'). Handsel Day was the first Monday of each year when small Christmas gifts were placed in boxes for the apprentices. This is also the origin of the **Christmas Boxes** which employers the world over still distribute to staff and customers every year.

Burning the Candle at Both Ends is often used to describe people exhausting themselves by getting up early for work and then playing (or working) hard, late into the night. (At least I am guilty of only one of those.) In bygone days, before electricity could keep us illuminated all night long, clerks and tradesmen working after dark would often secure their candles in the middle (horizontally) and then light them at both ends. This would give them enough light to work by, but not for very long, so they would have to work harder and faster in these conditions. This gave rise to the expression that we still use today.

If we carry out a task in a **Half-assed** fashion then we are not concentrating fully or putting much thought or effort into it. The original expression was 'half adze' and had been used for centuries prior to the slight variation in pronunciation. An adze was, and still is, an axe-like tool with a curved blade that was used by carpenters to shape wood. The story goes that if you were wealthy and could afford to pay for fine furniture, you would buy pieces that had been finished completely, including the back and other unseen areas, such as inside drawers.

However, if you were buying economically, you were likely to find all the unseen areas, such as those placed next to a wall, were unfinished and plain. These cheaper jobs were known as 'half adze' work. A similar expression in regular use is **Half Baked**. If an idea has not been thought through completely, it might be likened to bread that has not been sufficiently baked through and needs to be finished off. To avoid association with the undesirable term, bakers now produce 'part-baked' bread, instead of the original 'half-baked', meaning customers can go home and finish it off themselves.

I Wouldn't Touch It with a Barge Pole is an expression we use when we want to keep something, or even a person, as far from us as possible, certainly further than arm's length. But the 'barge pole' is a relatively new addition to the idiom. To quote from a poem included in *Wit Restored* (1658): 'Without a

payre of tongs no man will touch her.' Tongs are the tool used to put logs on to a fire or pick up dirty objects and were a common household item during the 17th century. Charles Dickens popularized that phrase in *Hard Times* (1854): 'I was so ragged and dirty you wouldn't have touched me with a pair of tongs.' It was at the turn of the 19th/20th century that the idiom changed. Popular with public schoolboys at the time was the phrase **Barging In** (see next entry). The same schoolboys, in an adaptation of the phrase found in Dickens, used 'barge pole' as the more derogatory term – barge poles (the long, sturdy wooden poles used for steering canal barges) being somewhat longer than tongs.

Barging In on something or someone is to intrude upon or abruptly interrupt a situation. Not quite naval in origin, the phrase does have a watery derivation. Since the development from the 17th century onwards of the English waterways, which prior to the railway network linked most major towns and cities, the boats used on them have been flat-bottomed barges. Due to the cumbersome handling of these vessels, collisions were commonplace and by the late 1800s schoolboys used the term 'barge in/into' for bumping into or 'hustling' somebody. By the turn of the century, the phrase had become widespread, having acquired its current meaning of to interrupt without invitation or to hassle somebody.

*

It's **All Grist to the Mill** is an expression we use for anything that might be able to turn us a profit. For example, a farmer might make a healthy sum out of selling a certain crop. But there may be more to be made by also selling leftover leaves and vegetable stalks to the pig farmer next door, and even more to be had by selling his horse manure to the local fruit farmer. All these little extra profits in any industry are known as 'grist to the mill'. 'Grist' is in fact the name given by the millers to the actual quantity of grain that can be put through the mill at any one time. In this literal sense, 'all grist to the mill' means everything will be ground, sawdust and all, with no leftovers and therefore maximum profit.

Any great work of art can be acknowledged as a **Masterpiece**. The expression is not restricted just to the visual arts either and can be traced to the Netherlands, to around 1580. Originally a craftsman, artist, writer or musician would mark the end of their training period and apprenticeship by producing a work reflecting their new status as 'master of the guild'. This one piece of work was called the 'master piece' and the phrase has been applied to exceptional creations ever since.

*

To be **Given the Mitten** is to be dismissed from your place of work or from an elected position. The phrase was widely used between the 19th and 20th centuries although it has largely been replaced now by **Being Fired** or **Given the Sack** (see next entry). A practice that began in the late 1500s consisted of a notice of dismissal being sent to a person in the form of a 'mittimus'. The word derives from the Latin verb *mittere*, meaning 'to send (away)'. During the 19th century, the phrase was used in a slightly different way, being applied to a gentleman jilting his beloved by giving her 'the mitten', or sending her away. Later in the century, the phrase reverted to its original sense of dismissing somebody from a job.

Being Fired. Prior to the invention of toolboxes, all English crafts- and tradesmen carried their tools around in a sack. Hence to be **Given the Sack** (in the sense of the sack being 'given back' to you) meant being discharged from employment, the worker either carrying his tools home or on to his next job. However, miners who were caught stealing coal, copper or tin (depending on the mine) would have their tools confiscated and burnt at the pit head in front of the other shift workers, a punishment that became known as 'firing the tools' or 'being fired'. This obviously meant the banished offender would be unable to find other work and repeat his 'crime' elsewhere. Other trades soon adopted the practice and the phrase 'being fired' quickly established itself as part of the English language. In a military context, the expression for being fired is 'discharged from duty' or 'dishonourable discharge'. Either way, you are out on your ear (to coin a phrase).

The **Graveyard Shift** is the time a person works when the workplace is at its quietest. Usually this is overnight, although it can be at other times of minimum activity, such as in restaurants and bars on a Monday lunchtime. The phrase was used widely during the Second World War when it was applied to the nightshift workers in the munitions factories. Since then, the phrase has been applied to other trades and professions. Journalists and news broadcasters have a 'graveyard shift', for example, which is often simply manning the phones overnight should any big news story break. The original graveyard shift was the job of the overnight guards in the quiet cemeteries who were on the look-out for grave robbers or even a **Dead Ringer** (see entry and **Skeleton in the Cupboard**).

Not to Care/Give a Tinker's Dam is used to express complete and abject lack of interest in a subject, believing it to be worthless. This has nothing to do with the word 'damn' or 'damnation', as is sometimes believed. A tinker is a type of traveller or gypsy who used to roam the countryside in his caravan looking for casual work, often repairing old pots, pans and kettles in exchange for food and clothing.

The tinker would plug a hole in a pan by surrounding it with a wall of clay, although he sometimes used bread for the purpose, and this was known as a 'dam'. Hot solder was then poured in and allowed to set, plugging the gap. Once this had gone hard, the tinker's dam would be broken off and thrown away as it was now useless, which is how the phrase became applied throughout the countryside to anything of absolutely no value or interest whatsoever.

To **Put Your Shoulder to the Wheel** means to add your effort to a joint task, as you will benefit in the long term. This is an expression first recorded in 1692 and calls to mind the horse-drawn carriage. Before the invention of **Tarmac** (see entry), it was common for a carriage to become stuck in the mud. When this happened, the driver would ask his passengers to help shift the carriage by disembarking and 'putting their shoulder to the wheel'. Royalty, nobility, gentry or otherwise, they would all have to lend a hand as there was no chance of the driver shifting it on his own.

A **Navvy** is a manual worker or labourer employed on a casual basis for a fixed period of time, often moving around the country, as building projects were completed and new ones began. During the Industrial Revolution, teams of manual labourers were employed throughout England to build the canal waterways, followed by the railway system. The canals were known as 'navigation networks' at the time and all the men employed to dig them termed 'navigators'. The word was soon abbreviated to 'navvy' and applied to anybody providing labour on the networks, whether water or rail.

To be all at **Sixes and Sevens** means to be in a state of disorder, unable to complete a task effectively. This is one of those wonderful old phrases still very much in use today but whose origin goes back a long way, none of us having any idea why it became so popular. The story is that in 1327 two of the great livery companies, the Skinners and the Merchant Taylors, each received their charter within a few days of the other. But an argument immediately broke out as to which of the two firms was to be placed at number six in the order of companies going on processions in the City of London, and which would be the seventh. The matter was resolved when it was suggested each company should share the coveted number six position by swapping places every year. This went on until 1484 when the masters of both firms submitted the matter to the then Mayor of London, Sir Robert Billesden, for his judgement. Rather than getting bogged down in all the rights and wrongs of the affair, Billesden decided a simple solution would be for the masters and wardens of both companies to entertain each other to dinner once a year, as well as continuing to alternate their places on the processions. How typically English.

The **Men in Grey Suits** are the faceless bureaucrats or administrators who govern and control many aspects of our lives without proper accountability. This expression was first used by the Beatle John Lennon when the world-famous band formed their own company, the Apple Organization, in the 1960s. Lennon was quoted at the time as saying: 'This is an attempt to wrestle control from the men in suits.' It was in the early 1990s, when Margaret Thatcher was eased from power by her own party, that much was made in the press about the nameless 'men in grey suits' who had engineered her dismissal from behind the scenes.

ALL AMERICAN

A **Lynch Mob** is a group of people determined to take the law into their own hands and dispense summary justice, initially in the form of beatings and then executions by hanging. A **Lynching** and to **Lynch** a person are obviously connected terms, but in fact arose after the expression 'lynch mob'. These mobs (vigilante groups of men) in the southern states of America were as much a part of life in the late 19th century as the cowboys were. In ten states alone, authorities recorded 2,805 deaths at the hands of the mobs between 1882 and 1930. Of the victims 2,500 were black, hanged without trial by white lynch mobs.

Over a hundred years earlier, Colonel James Lynch of Bedford County and Captain William Lynch of Pittsville County were struggling to keep law and order in their respective states, and so in 1780

William Lynch made a formal agreement with his neighbours to deal with troublesome and lawless men in their area. He formed a group of men and declared that if the trouble-makers 'will not desist from their evil practices, we shall inflict such corporeal punishment on him or them, as to us shall seem adequate to the crime committed or the damage sustained'. 'Corporeal' (now 'corporal') punishment meant a horsewhipping and beating at that point, rather than execution. The group became known as 'Lynch's Mob' and this eventually led to the term being used in the *New-England Magazine* in October 1835 as the title of an article: 'The Inconveniences of Being Lynched'. A piece from 1843 in the *New York Daily Express* tells of a person who was 'lately taken from his house at night by some of his neighbours and severely lynched [thrashed]'. And so the lynch mob was born.

A **Yankee** or a **Yank** is US and European slang for an American. Originally the Native American Indians used the words *yengees*, *yanghis* and *yankees* to describe English and French settlers. Dutch settlers who arrived at the turn of the 18th century immediately began to use the word to describe all Americans, and the nickname became established after Jonathan Hastings, a farmer in Cambridge, New York state, used it in 1713 to describe his products as 'genuine American-made and cannot be bettered

. . . Yankee Butter, the best in the world . . . Yankee leather, the best available', etc.

The expression **Jumping the Gun** would mean we have started a task too soon, before others were considered ready. Often thought to have emerged in the field of athletics, where events begin at the sound of a starting pistol, the idiom may in fact be military in origin. On the battlefield, the artillery would be placed at the front of the army with the infantry waiting behind them for the order to be given to attack the enemy on foot. However, some ill-disciplined troops would quite literally jump over the guns and attack before being ordered to do so. A second theory reminds us of the Oklahoma Land Grab during the 1800s. Settlers would gather at the state border and were not allowed to move into the area and make a land claim until a cannon was fired to give the signal. Those who jumped the gun would be shot by US troops.

Catch-22 is an expression used to explain a situation where a person has no choice at all, and is similar in meaning to **Apply Morton's Fork** (see entry). The phrase began to be used in America following the publication of Joseph Heller's book of the same name in September 1961. In the story, Heller's central character, a Second World War bomber pilot called Captain John Yossarian, believed he could be relieved from active duty by claiming insanity.

Although it was noted that in attempting to avoid any further missions Yossarian was in fact proving he had all his wits about him after all, as the following extract shows: 'There was only one catch and that was Catch-22 which specified that any concern for one's own safety, in the face of dangers that were real and immediate, was the process of a rational mind.' But the idiom we use today could have been quite different as Heller originally called his book *Catch-18*, only altering it to avoid confusion with Leon Uris's novel about the Warsaw ghetto uprising, *Mila-18*, which was published in 1953. *Catch-22* quickly attracted a cult following and became the draft dodgers' bible during the Vietnam War in the 1960s.

Close But No Cigar is another American expression that has crossed the Atlantic and is used widely in Britain. It is said to describe an act or event coming very close to succeeding, but not quite close enough, and is thought to come from the custom of lighting a big cigar to celebrate a major success. For its origin, however, we need to look to the wandering fairs and circuses touring 19th-century America and entertaining people along the way. Many sideshows would offer the public the prize of a large Havana cigar for winning such competitions as shooting the spots off a playing card, or smacking a mallet against a pad to try to make a nail shoot up the pole and ring a bell located at the very top. Despite the obvious fun they were all having back in the 1800s, many would have been disappointed to come close but not actually win the cigar.

The Best Thing Since Sliced Bread is a metaphor meaning the very best of something. In 1912, Otto Frederick Rohwedder, of Iowa, USA, began work on a bread-slicing machine. The machine took time to perfect, mainly due to the difficulty in keeping sliced bread fresh, but in 1927 a waxed paper bag solved that problem for him. The first slicing machine was installed the following year at the Chillicothe Baking Company, owned by a friend of Otto's called M. Frank Bench, and on 7 July 1928 the first sliced loaf was sold. Known as the 'Sliced Kleen Maid Bread', the product was an instant success and customers were delighted with the neat and even slices, which were so easy to use.

A new era had dawned and Otto became known as the father of sliced bread. However, during the Second World War the then agricultural secretary, Claude Wickard, banned sales of sliced bread (as an unnecessary manufacturing process) in an effort to hold down prices as rationing was introduced. The British government soon followed suit and consumers protested at the loss of one of their favourite products. But no sooner had the war ended than sliced bread returned and was once again available all over America, Britain and Europe, to the delight of everybody. It was then that advertisers, keen to link their products with the popularity of sliced bread, coined the expression we use today. Although this raises another question: what was the best thing *before* sliced bread?

To **Eat Crow** is an expression of American origin used to describe personal discomfort, humiliation and embarrassment. Similar to the English idiom **Eating Humble Pie** (see entry), the phrase has its root in the folklore of the late 19th century and a story that was apparently reported in the *Atlanta Constitution* in 1888. According to the story, during an armistice of the Anglo-American War (1812–14), a New Englander made the mistake of crossing the English lines, while out hunting, and shot dead a crow. An unarmed English officer heard of this and resolved to punish the offender. He found the American and praised him for his marksmanship, gaining his confidence enough to be given the weapon for a trial shot himself. At this point, the officer advised the American he was trespassing and turned the gun on him, forcing him to take a bite out of the dead crow, which the trembling American duly did. When the officer was satisfied the American was suitably humiliated, he gave back the weapon and told him to return to his own lines. At which point, the American turned the tables and forced the hapless Brit to eat the remainder of the crow. Which is the part of the story I just do not believe: who would be that stupid to give the gun back? Mind you, on the other hand . . .

*

A **Hooker** is a term applied on both sides of the Atlantic to describe a prostitute. There are two suggested origins for the word. The first is a location in New York called Corlear's Hook, known locally as 'The Hook', which was a place where ladies of the night could apply their skills in the latter part of the 19th century. Secondly, we are introduced to General Joseph Hooker, who may also have had a hand in it during the American Civil War when a certain area of Washington DC became known as 'Hooker's Division'. It is also known that the general had an established and loyal group of camp followers (see **Camp It Up**).

The expression **Knocked into a Cocked Hat** is used when something, or someone, has been soundly defeated and proved to be inferior to another. This is an American phrase which some suggest is connected to the headgear worn by Puritans in the 17th century. They wore their hats with the brim turned up (cocked) on three sides, giving their heads a strange triangular appearance that was ridiculed by many. It is said that comedians and jesters of the day would remove the hat of a fellow actor and knock it into a 'cocked hat shape' to show themselves to be dominant and superior, much to the delight of the crowds. After all, a hat so drastically pushed out of shape is good for nothing much but laughter. However, the phrase could apply equally well to the headgear worn by American army field officers in the 18th and 19th centuries, who were issued with three-cornered (tricorne) hats that became known as 'cocked hats'. They also had the brim turned up on three sides, giving them a comical look that would have exposed them to mockery. A further suggestion indicates that the origin might lie in the popular game of skittles, of which the American version only used three pins, making the target look like a cocked hat. To knock all the pins over with one ball became known as 'knocking the pins into a cocked hat (shape)'. But that explanation seemed a little thin to me, especially when further research revealed that the expression appeared in print for the first time in 1833, whereas there was no reference to three-pin skittles until 1856. It looks like the joke of humiliating a man by knocking his hat out of shape to resemble an early Puritan's, or the army headgear that was so ridiculed, might well be the root of the expression.

To **Knock Off Work for the Day** means it is the end of your shift and time to go home. Research suggests that the source of the expression can be found in the Deep South during the days when pious white American settlers believed it was God's will that they should make slaves of black Africans.

Apparently the men who used to beat out the rhythm for oarsmen to pull in a co-ordinated fashion (on river boats transporting the workers to and from plantations) would have a special knock indicating when it was time to change shifts. The phrase was not recorded in Britain prior to 1902, but it is thought that in Victorian factories and workhouses knocking a mallet or a hammer on to a workbench would signal the end of each working shift.

To be **Moseying About** is an American expression that found its way across the Atlantic during the mid 19th century. It suggests someone wandering around in an unhurried manner in search of something, perhaps in a bookshop or a craft market. The early Spanish settlers to the New World introduced many words, including *vamos*, which may be translated as 'let's go' and is the origin of the word 'vamoose', meaning 'to depart hurriedly'. The word 'mosey' is a corruption and slight extension of the Spanish word by English settlers.

Nothing Is Certain Except Death and Taxes is an expression commonly used to illustrate that any event could have more than one outcome; nothing is guaranteed in life. Of American origin, the phrase is a direct quote from one of the founding fathers, whose signature appears on the Declaration of Independence – Benjamin Franklin no less. In 1789, political opponents were pressing Franklin for a prediction of how the new constitution would work for the American people. Within a week, part of Franklin's reply had made headlines all across the new country, and subsequently in Britain: 'Our Constitution is in actual operation and everything appears to promise that it will last; but in this world nothing is certain but death and taxes.'

When something finally **Peters Out**, it has gradually ceased to exist, rather than suddenly ended without notice or forewarning. During the Californian gold rush of the mid 19th century, the explosive used to open up the seams in a gold mine was gunpowder, a combination of charcoal, sulphur and saltpetre (or 'saltpeter' in US spelling – hence 'peter'), and once a seam had been fully mined and exploited it was known to be 'petering out', which is how the expression became widely used in America and then crossed the Atlantic to Britain during the late 1800s.

To **Send Somebody Up the River** is an American expression meaning to imprison. New York's Sing Sing Jail lies up the Hudson River from New York City and convicts were sent by boat to be incarcerated there. Since 1891, the phrase has been used in the States in respect of jailing a person.

A **Ten Gallon Hat** is the cowboy hat American ranch workers and cowboys would wear to shield them from the heat of the sun as they went about their work on the plains. It was John B. Stetson (1830–1906) who popularized the broad-brimmed hat when his company, founded in Philadelphia in 1865, began producing the Stetson or, as it was sometimes called, the John B. The nickname 'ten gallon hat' was introduced in the late 1800s as a reflection on its capacity to carry large quantities of water, although a slight exaggeration had been made as nothing like that volume could fit inside the crown, certainly not in brains anyway. The expression passed into wider use in America, followed by Britain, as a result of the popular westerns produced by American film companies during the 1920s. As for the reference to ten gallons of water, it is possible the idea stems from an advert the Stetson Company produced at the time showing a cowboy standing beside his horse as it drank water from the upturned hat.

To **Pass the Buck** is an easy thing to do, as it means avoiding taking responsibility yourself by passing the matter along to others for them to deal with it. In the American Mid West, during the 19th century, the game of poker was one of the most popular pastimes of all. As part of the game, each player has to take a turn at dealing, which at times is worth avoiding as it means declaring the first stake (bet). Back in the days of the Wild West, the most common knife available was known as a buckhorn knife (so called because the handle was carved from the horn of a buck deer). As all cowboys and ranchers carried them around, one of them would be placed in front of whoever was due to deal the next hand, and in games where the stakes were running too high for a player, he may opt out of his turn at dealing by passing the buckhorn knife on to the next player. But even if he did choose to play, he still avoided the responsibility of setting the bets next time around by passing the buck along. Later, at the great casinos and gaming houses in Las Vegas, a silver dollar was used in place of a knife and that is how the slang term for a US dollar (**Buck**) arose. The expression 'pass the buck' was known by 1865 and the first recorded use was by Mark Twain in 1872. Later on, in 1945, President Truman famously had a plaque made and placed on his desk in the Oval Office of the White House. It read **The Buck Stops Here**, a clear declaration that he was prepared to accept responsibility for all the decisions taken during his term of office. Later presidents Carter, Ford and Nixon all copied the idea, and the expression has since been widely used.

THE RULING CLASSES

The word **Boss** has some interesting applications. It derives from the Dutch word *baas*, translated as 'master', and is used to describe any person in charge, hence the expression 'to boss somebody around'. But **Boss-eyed** has no Dutch connection at all and derives instead from the Old English dialect version of the word 'boss', meaning 'to miss'. The straw 'boss' (derived from the same Old English word) on an archery target forms the mat-like backing the actual target is pinned to. Any archer missing his target had 'bossed his shot', meaning his arrow had hit the boss (i.e. the backing) and not the target, and thus he was regarded as 'boss-eyed'.

To be going at **Full Tilt** means to be performing something at top speed, whether sailing, running, riding, driving, etc., or it could refer to machinery operating as fast as it will possibly go. In medieval England, jousting was known as 'tilting' and knights on horseback would charge at each other at high speed, lances aimed at their opponents. The phrase derives from the old English word *tealt*, which means 'unstable' or 'leaning'.

We use the expression **Blue Blooded** to describe people who are from royal or aristocratic families – those who consider themselves socially superior. In 711, the Moors invaded Spain for the first time and for many centuries much of the country was under Moorish rule. During the Middle Ages, fair-skinned Europeans called all Asian people, and indeed darker-skinned Mediterranean folk, 'Moors', and in Spain members of the aristocracy, with particularly pale skin as the result of never intermarrying with 'Moors', were termed *Sangre Azul*, which may be translated literally as 'Blue Blood'. This is because the veins under the skin appear much bluer in paler-skinned people, leading to the belief that the white Spanish nobility must be fundamentally different from the Moors – whom the aristocracy considered to be socially inferior to themselves – and hence that their blood must also be blue in colour.

To be **Born with a Silver Spoon in Your Mouth** is to be born into a wealthy family. It was traditional for godparents to present a newborn baby with the gift of a silver spoon, thereby providing the child's first 'taste' of wealth and good fortune. It could be said, however, that those born into a rich family had no need to wait for a godparent to make such a gift as they already had great wealth. They had been born with their own 'silver spoon', as it were. A similar expression, although no longer in use, is **Born in the Purple**. According to an ancient custom, Byzantine emperors made sure that all of their successors were born in a special room decorated solely in imperial purple, representing their royal status. For a thousand years, the expression 'born in the purple' (room) was used to describe any royal or noble birth, but alas, the purple people have not been heard of since 1453 when their empire finally collapsed and, no doubt, their nobility was marooned.

A **Right-hand Man** is generally regarded to be an influential person's second in command, someone who is both indispensable and heavily relied upon. Traditionally, a senior servant or assistant would be given the privilege of sitting or standing on the right-hand side of his master. This was not only a show of faith and trust, as from that position the servant could disable his master's sword arm (usually his right) and overcome him with ease, but also because the servant was in the best place to defend his master. Occupying such a position held great importance during the Middle Ages because the 'right-hand man' was seen to be as necessary to his master as the latter's own right hand.

An Englishman's Home Is His Castle is taken to mean a person's home is private, sacrosanct and to be protected at all costs. This is an expression that derives from the Middle Ages and an old law that prevented any person from forcing entry to a private dwelling to carry out an arrest or to seize goods and chattels. That same law prevented the bailiffs of the high sheriff from breaking in and helping themselves to a person's goods, and it is still the case that no bailiff is allowed to enter a private dwelling without first obtaining a court order.

To be **Given the Seal of Approval** means that a project or an activity has been checked and given the go-ahead by those in authority. Seals, whether of wood, bone or metal, have been used to authenticate documents for over two thousand years, pressed into a variety of materials, including clay, mud and wax. The coat of arms of an individual or official body, such as the government or the army, used to be engraved on to a signet ring, and this would then be pressed into the wax sealing a document closed. The idea was to show the person on the receiving end that they were in receipt of a genuine, official document. Any document with the king's seal pressed into the wax was to be taken very seriously indeed, especially if the seal had also been made under the last line, indicating the proposal outlined in the document had been fully approved. The practice still continues to this day, although officials now use a rubber stamp to approve papers. Hence the expression **Rubber Stamped** may be applied in exactly the same way as being 'given the seal of approval'.

We now understand our **Birthday Suit** to be one of complete nakedness, suggesting this was the 'suit' we were born in. That's hard to argue with, but the original 'birthday suit', or at least the one the expression referred to in the first place, is a specially commissioned suit of clothes worn by all royal courtiers on the reigning monarch's birthday. While that tradition has long since died out, the expression remains with us.

To **Lionize** someone is to treat them as a celebrity and to show them off in front of others. From 1834, all exotic animals gifted to the King of England would be kept and displayed at the Tower of London. Such creatures from far-off continents included leopards, bears, wolves, lynxes and the star attraction, the African lions. The great and the good of London society and royal circles would often entertain important guests at the Tower, and any celebrities might find themselves the centre of attention during such gatherings and sometimes put on display by their hosts – 'shown off', just like the lions.

To **Keep a Stiff Upper Lip** is a phrase used to encourage a cool, calm and collected response in the face of danger. It is an admirably British quality characterized by the Victorian empire builders, particularly the military, who would manage to control their facial features, especially the lips, so as not to betray any emotional turmoil within. The expression epitomizes courage and an indomitable spirit in the face of adversity. After all, it wouldn't do for an officer and a gentleman to show any feelings when his men are being torn to ribbons by the enemy before his very eyes, now would it? 'Come along, men, keep up the good work for queen and country – we have the flag of democracy flying on our side. And it's nearly time for afternoon tea, don't you know.'

A **Battle Royal** is a zealously fought contest, sporting or otherwise. It can be waged on the football pitch, the terraces or between warring factions of all kinds, on battlefields either literal or metaphorical. They are always free-for-alls and result in general mayhem. The original term became part of the English language during the 1670s via the obsession at that time with cock fighting. It was such a popular pastime that people of every class, even the aristocracy and members of the royal families across Europe, would send their prized cocks into the fray. The royal cocks were usually the most magnificent of all and consequently often the best of the fighting birds. Cock fighting would take place in stages. In the first instance, 16 birds would be dropped into a pit and then fight each other randomly – usually they would scrap with the nearest bird – until eight of them had been pecked to pieces and were no longer able to continue. The surviving eight would then be sent into battle again for round two, until only four remained, and so on until the two most resilient cocks fought in the final. By that time, even the champion cocks were beginning to wilt but, spurred on by the crowd, would fight to the death. The royal cocks would usually wage the fiercest, and subsequently most talked about, battles. They truly were battle royals.

To be **On the Side of the Angels** means to be in agreement with those who are perceived to be beyond reproach, the so-called ruling classes and the morally sound. In other words, they think you are always right. This is a phrase that can be traced directly to a speech given by Queen Victoria's favourite politician and a former prime minister, Benjamin Disraeli. At a convention in Oxford, addressing the complicated issue of evolution, Disraeli was invited to speak. Not one to miss an opportunity to present himself to as many people as possible, he readily agreed and yet didn't appear to have much of a clue about the subject in question. During his speech, Disraeli declared himself opposed to Darwin's theory that our fore-fathers were in fact apes and insisted man was a direct descendant of God himself. 'Is man an ape or an angel?' he cried. 'I, my lord, am on the side of the angels.' I wonder if he also believed in Father Christmas or the Tooth Fairy.

*

The Great and the Good of this land are those who are considered (certainly by themselves) as socially superior to the rest of us. Basically they are members of the aristocracy, government, leading business figures and anybody else of influence. Such was the state of the English class system until towards the end of the 20th century that a list of names actually existed and there were still 4,500 people on it as recently as 1984. Prior to that, those administering 'the list' had been trying to include more people from outside London and the Southeast, involve more women and people younger than 40. This happened after Lord Rothschild famously remarked that the list contained only '53-year-old men who live in the South East, have the right accent and belong to the Reform Club'. Such was their control over the rest of our lives that on one occasion they actually nominated two of their own kind for important roles in public service who were, in fact, already dead. In the 1950s, the Treasury, which was responsible for maintaining the list, had a division known as 'the G&G'.

When someone is on their **High Horse** they appear dismissive and aloof, as if looking down upon the rest of us. Medieval knights and other noblemen used to wear magnificent suits of armour, which would weigh around 300 pounds. As a result, they could only ride specially bred horses, which were much larger than normal and hence able to carry the extra weight. It was not uncommon for noble gentlemen to ride through English towns looking down upon the locals on their ordinary-sized nags. Later, politicians would parade in ceremonial processions mounted on outsized horses, leading to the expression 'he is up on his high horse again'. The phrase appears for the first time in James Kelly's *Collection of Scottish Proverbs* (1721). In a similar vein, we might tell someone to **Come Off It** (meaning that we are not taken in by them), which is an expression that began life as 'come down off your high horse'.

FOOD FOR THOUGHT

When you are **Given the Cold Shoulder** it is obvious you are not welcome any more, so must be on your way. This phrase can be traced to the great banquets of medieval England. During the feasts, which usually lasted for days, sometimes even weeks, the host (perhaps an English lord or a prominent knight) would provide sumptuous meals of venison, beef, game and trout. All this would be washed down with copious amounts of wine and ale while travelling musicians, dancers and jesters would entertain a gathering of noblemen and women, and possibly royalty too. It was customary at the time for the host to signal the end of the festivities by asking his cooks to serve slices from shoulders of cold beef, mutton or pork. It was regarded as far more in keeping with his status to send the message in that way rather than for him to visit all his many guests in person (sometimes in their hundreds) to inform them the party was over. This tradition also passed over to the commoners, who would serve guests who had outstayed their welcome, from a cold shoulder of mutton. These days to be 'given the cold shoulder' is perceived as rude and unkind, although in medieval times it was regarded as a civilized and polite gesture. In fact, if the history books are to be believed, it was probably the most civilized part of the whole, over-the-top banqueting scene. An extension of the phrase is to be **Cold Shouldered**, which is also widely used today.

If something (or someone) **Saves Your Bacon** then it prevents a loss on a large scale, whether financially, professionally, romantically, etc. – or it could perhaps even mean your life had been saved. Bacon and other pig-related terms have been used as metaphors for people since as long ago as the 11th century. During the Middle Ages, pork was one of the few types of meat widely available and affordable throughout England, and for many it was the only meat they had to eat. This led to derision from both the aristocracy and the rich Norman lords, who, for example, would call Saxons 'hogs'. Writers and other artists have often used similar derogatory terms for country folk, such as 'swine' and 'pig' as well as 'hog'. Hence a country worker was known as a 'chaw-bacon' (meaning 'bacon chewer' – or 'carrot cruncher', as the term is better known these days).

Regardless of this, farmers and land workers guarded their bacon stores very carefully, especially as dogs and other wild animals roamed the land looking for such food to scavenge. A hungry farm worker would thus always be relieved if somebody had 'saved his/her bacon'.

To get yourself **Tanked Up** is to be rolling drunk of a Friday or Saturday night – or, for that matter, at any time. This phrase takes us back to the taverns and inns of medieval England when drinks were served in clay tankards. If a customer drank vast quantities of ale and then passed out, they were known as 'tankard'. Although many of the English youth of today use a word that rhymes with it to describe the same kind of state, it is easy to see how, over time, 'tankard' became corrupted to 'tanked up'.

The term **Lager Louts** describes young people whose sole weekend ambition is to drink as much alcohol as they can, go to a football match and start a fight. Such cultural pastimes became popular in Britain during the 1980s as employment began to rise and memories of the recession of the late 1970s blurred in a haze of hangovers. With more disposable income available, the Thatcher government encouraged consumer spending and suddenly the high streets were full of drunken youngsters. It was Simon Walters, the political correspondent of that lager lout 'bible' the *Sun*, who coined the phrase that made

headlines – literally as well as metaphorically – at the time. On 13 April 1989, he owned up to it in a letter to the *Independent*: 'It dates back to last August when the Home Office referred to the "lager culture" among young trouble makers. From that I came up with the term lager lout to give it more of a meaning.'

When something **Has Got Legs** it means it is of good and reliable quality and will last for a long time. For example, if a book has sold very well during a busy Christmas period, and then finds itself being serialized by a national newspaper in January for six months, it could quite easily be described as 'having legs now' (i.e. longevity). The wine industry is well known for the apparently absurd procedures wine tasters adopt when deciding if a certain bottle is good, average or indifferent. But there is a very good reason for the sniff/swirl/spit method of wine tasting that makes for such humorous viewing on television. First a taster needs to check the clarity of the wine and then smell it to verify that there are no re-fermentation or bacterial problems. Secondly, the wine should be swirled around the glass as this will leave trails of wine appearing to run back down towards the main pool of liquid – known in the trade as 'legs' (or 'tears'). Pronounced 'legs' on the side of the glass are said to indicate a high level of alcohol in the wine and perhaps increased residual sugar content, and so to declare a wine has got 'great legs' is to compliment and recommend it. The legs in question are due to what is known as the Gibbs-Marangoni effect, in which ethanol evaporates from the wine, wetting the inside of the glass above the liquid. In the absence of ethanol, the surface tension of the alcohol increases and so it contracts to minimize the surface area. This in turn brings more ethanol-laden liquor to the top and that starts to form the legs, which in fact are running upwards and hence defying gravity. The legs then form at the highest point, since there is less ethanol there, before becoming large enough to roll back down again under their own weight, and a manner of convection flow is created in the glass. After all that, I am not so sure whether it really matters whether we spit or swallow the wine because the taste on the palate will remain much the same either way.

*

Not Cutting the Mustard is an expression used to describe something or someone not meeting a certain standard. One suggested origin for the phrase is American and dates to the early 1900s when 'mustard' became used as a slang term for 'the genuine article' – the best of anything. For example, a favourite horse in a race might have it said of him: 'See that nag over there; he's mustard he is.' By contrast, 'not cutting the mustard' might be used to describe a badly performing employee or member of a team. Mustard plants grow very low to the ground and have notoriously strong stems, making them one of the hardest plants to harvest. Traditionally, a farmer or farm worker needed to spend day after day bent double, or even on their knees, engaged in hard manual labour to reap the plant. Once a worker became too old to work in these conditions, they were known to be 'unable to cut the mustard plant', and either moved on to lighter duties or had to stop working altogether.

A second, and possibly more likely, source for the expression takes us to the Bible and Jesus's 'Parable of the Mustard Seed' (Matthew 13:31–2): 'The kingdom of heaven is like to a grain of mustard seed, which a man took, and sowed in his field:/ Which indeed is the least of all seeds: but when it is grown, it is the greatest among herbs, and becometh a tree, so that the birds of the air come and lodge in the branches thereof.' The suggestion here is that mustard 'trees' will grow to be vast and sturdy, like cedar trees or redwood. For centuries, mustard was considered a powerful remedy for ill-ness. The Romans introduced it to Britain in the first instance and by the tenth century it had become one of the most important medicinal plants, pro-viding cures for headache and bronchial congestion, to name but a few. It is quite possible the Romans introduced the phrase 'past cutting the mustard tree' as a reference to a person being too sick to warrant someone going to the effort of cutting the huge trees, mentioned in the parable, to obtain a cure.

The expression passed into wider use throughout England and America with the song 'Too Old to Cut the Mustard', performed by Marlene Dietrich and Rosemary Clooney in 1952. Oh well, it happens to all of us in the end.

To **Broach a Subject** is to start a conversation in a general way with one or more people. The root of this term can be tracked down to the alehouses and hotels of London several centuries ago. In order to gain access to and draw ale from a new barrel, a barman would hammer a peg, known as a 'broach', into a hole at the base of the barrel. This was known as 'broaching the barrel', which started the beer flowing so the fun could begin.

To **Take the Cake** is an American expression, although also commonly used in the UK, meaning to be outrageous enough to deserve merit. A stunt pilot or racing driver, for example, might 'take the cake' for his audacity. It has been recorded that this phrase originated in the late 19th century among black slaves working on the southern plantations in America. It seems they devised a game whereby couples would parade arm in arm around a barn and were judged by the others on the style and grace of their walk. The winning couple would be given a cake as a prize and the most flamboyant and entertaining of them could expect to hear cries of 'they take the cake'. This pastime was known as the **Cakewalk**, which is also a well-known expression for something that is easy to achieve.

However, it is quite possible that the root of this expression goes back much earlier, to the Bible in fact. As missionaries converted large parts of Africa to Christianity, teaching from the Bible became widespread. For most inhabitants of the region it was likely to have been the only book they had ever read; thus its influence was profound. There is one story, for instance, telling how a biblical knight would be rewarded with a cake made of toasted cereal, sweetened with honey, if he was judged the most successful knight either in battle or in the workplace. There is strong evidence to suggest that African Americans adopted this reward after learning about the tale. However, anybody competing in the cakewalk who was considered rather too flamboyant and cheeky would be brought back down to earth by being awarded a biscuit instead. They had **Taken the Biscuit** (gone too far).

Going **Cold Turkey** is often considered to be the best way to wean a person off hard drugs, although the expression can also be applied to indicate how a person may feel in the absence of anything, from alcohol to chocolate and other foods that one might have to abstain from for dietary or health reasons. The expression was first recorded in the 1930s where several quotations can be found. The original idea was that a person withdrawing from using drugs would find their skin turning hard to the touch and translucent to look at, with goose pimples all over – like the skin of a plucked turkey. American Beat writer William Burroughs suggested in his book *Junkie* (1953) that human skin, during the period of withdrawal, resembles that of a turkey that has been plucked, then cooked and left to cool. Others believe the expression dates back to 1910 and makes a comparison between a meal of cold turkey, which requires virtually no preparation, and withdrawing from heavy drug use without preparation.

A **Bean Feast** is the expression commonly used for a company outing, usually a meal. It is a major 'get together' funded by an employer to promote harmony and goodwill among employees. In these days of political correctness, such outings are better known as 'bonding' or 'team-building' exercises, but originally they were recognized for what they actually were – a good old knees-up.

An annual outing would be arranged on special occasions such as an anniversary, at the end of the financial year or, more commonly, at Christmas. There are two suggestions as to how we began using the phrase 'bean feast', the first relating to the bean goose. These birds usually arrive in Britain in large numbers during the autumn and, centuries ago, they were what was served at Christmas before turkeys became the festive dish of choice. Known as the 'bean goose' because of the bean-shaped markings on its bill, the bird was easily available and relatively cheap, and therefore usually served to employees at the annual celebration, leading to the term 'bean feast'. A second suggestion insists the phrase has its roots in the 'beans and bacon' traditionally served with the goose. Either way, these work outings would invariably become rowdy affairs – proving nothing really changes over the years, if publisher parties are anything to go by. 'Bean feast' has in turn led to the word 'beano' or 'beaner' (bender) entering the language.

During the 17th century, a new fashion crossed the English Channel and it was called a **Picnic**. In France at the time, a new type of party had been introduced known as a *pique-nique* in which the guests would bring along a share of the food and wine so that the burden of providing would not be left to only one family. Consequently, these social get-togethers were often held in outdoor public places, and to this day the word is used to describe an outdoor meal, usually with friends.

Punch is a drink we are often served at picnics and it is one to be avoided at all costs. Some hosts delight in making a punch of the strongest alcohol available, which usually ends up tasting like it should be poured into the engine of a rusty tractor. During the early 1600s, as English explorers first made their way to the Indian sub-continent, one of their discoveries was a popular drink that consisted of five ingredients: water, sugar, spirits, spices and fruit juice. The Hindi word for five is *punch* and this is how the drink became known when it was served back in England throughout the social gatherings of the day. Unfortunately, in my experience, some people seem to delight in including paint stripper, paraffin and any leftover spirits, which is not the idea at all.

The word **Barbecue** began being used in England in the mid 1600s, meaning a wooden framework either for sleeping on (i.e. a bed) or, in a later application of the term, for storing meat on or laying fish out to be dried. It derives from the Spanish word *barbacoa*, or possibly from the same word in the West Indian Arawak language, both meaning 'wooden frame on posts'. On this framework a large animal would be turned from time to time and roasted over an open fire, which leads us to the word we use today to explain the English custom of standing out in the cold on a summer's afternoon eating burnt chicken and potato salad. There is an interesting modernization of the word; in aerospace technology there are two phrases used to describe the rotation of a space craft to allow the heat from the sun to be spread evenly over the surface in what has been described as a sort of 'log roll'. One is the 'barbecue mode' and the other the 'barbecue manoeuvre'.

A **Bistro** is a fast-food café, or at least it was until the ultra-fast-food outlets began to dominate our high streets in the 1970s – if you really can call any of what they sell 'food'. After the defeat of Napoleon at the Battle of Waterloo in 1815, troops from all over Europe began to occupy Paris, particularly the Russians. Naturally the French cafés were soon bustling with new visitors, trade was roaring and one of the most frequent shouts to be heard at the time was '*bweestra, bweestra*', which means 'quickly' in Russian. Hence the word soon became associated with cheap bars, small clubs and cafés.

'Welcome to my **Humble Abode**' is a cliché used by many on inviting a guest into their house for the first time. If that sort of contrived self-deprecation is not annoying enough, then it is especially annoying when there is nothing 'humble' about the house at all – the word deriving from the Latin *humilis*, meaning 'lowly'. Two famous books that have been turned into plays and films over the years are responsible for popularizing the phrase. The first is Jane Austen's *Pride and Prejudice* (1813), in which the clergyman Mr Collins (see also **Collins**) states: 'The garden in which stands my humble abode is separated only by a lane from Rosings Park, her ladyship's residence.' The second – taking us from the romantic vision of genteel country life to the grimness and poverty of industrial London – is Charles Dickens' *David Copperfield* (1850), in which the slimy Uriah Heep remarks: 'My mother is a very umble person. We live in an umble abode.'

Eating Humble Pie is to make an apology for some misdemeanour, usually having to accept humiliation in the process. The expression dates back to the Middle Ages and the banquet that would be held after a hunt. During the feast, the lord of the manor and his peers would be served the finest cuts of venison. But the entrails and offal, known at the time as 'umbles', would be baked into a pie and served to those of a lower standing or out of favour with the lord. It was common practice for people to be humiliated by finding themselves seated at the wrong end of the table and served 'umble pie'. In *David Copperfield* (1850), by Charles Dickens, Uriah Heep says at one point: 'I got to know what umbleness did and I took to it. I ate umble pie with an appetite.'

And that is how the phrase caught on throughout Britain.

A **Lush** is a person who drinks a little more than is good for them. It is a phrase that has been used regularly in America since the early 1800s, but the source can be found in London in the mid 18th century where 'lush' was a slang word for beer. At that time there was a club called the Harp Tavern, located in Russell Street near the Drury Lane Theatre, that was popular with actors and artists. In 1750, patrons formed the City of Lushington, a private members' club at the tavern, and their group appointed a chairman they termed 'the Lord Mayor' and a committee of four 'aldermen', who presided over the wards of Jupiter, Lunacy, Poverty and Suicide, Jupiter being the senior alderman named after the Roman god who presided over all 'human interest'. Drinkers were often known to turn night into day and their antics earned them the nickname of 'Lushes' or 'Lushers'. By 1790, the word 'lush' was in regular use to describe a heavy drinker or a drunk. Further expressions came and went, such as 'Alderman Lushington', which in 1810 referred to a drunk, and by the end of that century lush was firmly established as part of the language, although the City of Lushington had faded away by the early 1900s. Mind you, 150 years is not a bad stay in a pub is it? I would have been hoicked out of there by my ear years earlier.

To **Make No Bones** about a subject is to speak plainly without minding about causing offence; coming straight to the point, in other words. The origin of the expression can be found in the game of dice, which was once called 'bones' after the material they were carved from. Similarly, in Old French there was an expression that may be translated as 'sliding of dice' that was used to describe the act of softening something that has been said. Another expression, **You Can Pick the Bones Out of That** (uttered as a sort of challenge), suggests a piece of work is so good no errors will be found anywhere, just as you would find no bones in a perfect piece of meat or in a stew.

Not to Mince Your Words is to speak plainly, frankly and with brutal honesty. The phrase is always used in the negative sense, as in 'not to' – we never hear anybody complaining of someone 'mincing their words', after all (we're clearly all amenable to a spot of flattery or economizing with the truth). The first recorded use of the expression can be traced to Joseph Hall's *Cases of Conscience* (1649), making it one of our older sayings. Some things we are told are unpleasant and difficult to take in, and the allusion is drawn from butchers who mince cheaper cuts of meat, often full of bones and gristle, to make them easier to swallow and digest. It has always been felt that a person 'not mincing his/her words' is not making any effort to soften their impact.

A **Sirloin Steak** is not really an idiom at all, but the favoured part of a loin of beef, so why include it in *Shaggy Dogs and Black Sheep*? The reason for including it is because of a wonderful tale behind it, which takes us back to the 1500s and the great banquets of Henry VIII. There is no way, all these years later, of confirming the truth of this story, but folklore tells us that apparently the old tyrant enjoyed a feast in one of his castles to such an extent on one occasion that he actually bestowed a knighthood on a loin of beef he had dined on. And so, much to the great amusement of his court, the favoured cut became known thereafter as Sir Loin. (This may also be the reason we all enjoy a 'baron of beef' from time to time.) I would love that story to be true, but, sadly, it is far more likely that the origin of our favourite cut of beef comes from the French word *sur*, meaning 'over', and *longe*, meaning 'loin'. The sirloin is, after all, the 'upper' cut of the loin of beef.

To **Sign the Pledge** is an expression of American origin, meaning to give up drinking alcohol. The source of this phrase can be traced to the height of the Temperance Movement during the 19th century which encouraged drinkers wishing to give up alcohol to 'sign the temperance pledge' and make a public declaration never to touch the evil stuff again. It is something many of us do every Saturday or Sunday morning after overindulging the night before, but without the resolve to put it into action. Alcoholics Anonymous has now replaced the Temperance Movement on both sides of the Atlantic, although drinkers are still encouraged to 'sign the pledge' (if no longer literally), a phrase that has also widened to mean an open declaration of renouncing just about anything. Some researchers suggest the associated word **Teetotal** – also meaning to abstain from alcohol altogether – derives from the practice of drinking tea instead of beer and wines, but in fact we need to turn to the Temperance Movement once again. In 1836, the organization extended its ban on consuming hard liquor to include more moderate forms of alcoholic drink, such as beer, cider and wines. On all pledges prior to that, drinkers were invited to reveal how far they wanted to go in their vow of abstinence by placing one of two letters next to their signature on the pledge: 'M (Moderation)' or 'T (Total)'.

To have a **Finger in Every Pie** is commonly used to describe a person who has an interest in many things, especially to do with business. It would be easier to understand if the phrase read 'a finger in *making* every pie', which would rid us of the image of somebody going around poking their finger into other people's peach crumble, thereby suggesting an interfering meddler. The expression has been in use for over four hundred years and is applied to anybody with wide and varied business interests. It is also used by some people to describe themselves in an attempt to appear mysterious and interesting when in fact they've probably never had their finger in anybody's pie.

THE ANCIENT WORLD

Rubbing Salt into the Wound is to make a person's shame, or pain in an emotional sense, even worse than it already is. A commonly suggested source for the expression is nautical in origin. Once an errant sailor had been punished by flogging, his comrades would rub preserving salt into his wounds, making them much more painful but healing the injuries a good deal faster than if they had been left untended. This may very well be the origin of the phrase, but for another possible source, and an earlier one at that, we need to turn to an associated idiom. If someone is **Not Worth Their Salt** they are regarded as not very good at their job or a particular task. During the days of the Roman empire, salt was an expensive commodity and soldiers were actually paid partly in salt, which they carried with them in leather pouches. This form of payment was known as a *salarium*, from the Latin word *sal*, meaning 'salt'. Hence to be 'not worth one's salt' would mean being not worth paying (in salt). It is thus easy to see how the English word **Salary** also originates from the word *sal* (salt). Any Roman who had been injured in battle would have to rub part of his salt (i.e. his wages) into the wound to help the healing process. He would indeed be having a bad day.

Bread has long been part of our lives, not only important in our diet but also to the very fabric of our language. As long ago as 1000 BC the Egyptians had discovered the bread-making process and even stumbled upon the method of holding back a piece of dough from a daily batch, for the following day, to help leaven their bread, which is a process known to this day as 'sourdough'. Before long the Greeks were in on the act, often using bread as part of their currency, and the practice began to spread across Europe. After the Roman republic ceased to exist, the Roman satirist Juvenal coined the phrase **Bread and Circuses**, a term used even now to mean 'benefits and entertainments for placating the discontented'. In one of his satires (written around AD 100–128), Juvenal criticizes the decline of heroism among the Romans: 'there are only two things the people now anxiously desire – bread and circuses.' This was in direct response to administrators of the new Roman empire taking on the role of providing bread for the entire domain, partly as a form of currency, and staging vast gladiatorial events, chariot races and other athletic contests for the entertainment of the people. In both medieval England and Iraq, bread was also a recognized form of currency.

In the 1920s and 1930s, gangsters in Chicago and New York, who adopted some particularly colourful slang terms, used the expression 'sourdough' for counterfeit money, possibly as a result of their infiltration and extortion of the city bakeries. This led to the widespread use of the words 'bread' and **Dough** as slang for 'money' or, in the gangsters' case, 'genuine money'. In cockney rhyming slang, **Bread and Honey** is the term for money and **Brown Bread** is often used in place of the word 'dead'.

A Chip Off the Old Block describes a child who is just like their father or mother, in both appearance and character. The obvious reference is to a chip of wood taken from a larger block, suggesting the carpenter cut off a small piece of wood that was exactly the same in every way to the larger piece, except in size. However, we have to go back thousands of years for the root of the expression, which started life as 'a chip off the flint'. The Greek poet Theocritus – dubbed the 'creator of pastoral verse' as he wrote mainly about country life – used the saying as long ago as 270 BC and suggested it was Stone Age in origin.

A person termed **Janus Faced** is thought of as hypocritical. Janus was a Roman deity who, myth tells us, was responsible for the gates of heaven (his name deriving from the word for 'gate' – *ianua*). He had two faces, one in the usual position, like yours and mine, and one at the back of his head, enabling him to see in all directions at once. The inference was that Janus could see all sides of a situation, and was able to agree with each argument in turn. All hypocritical people are to this day regarded as **Two Faced** (like Janus). Janus has also given us the name for the month of January, a time of year that, like the god, looks in two directions – back to the Old Year and forward to the New.

A **Benchmark** is a level, or standard, of quality and performance. In the days of the great Greek and Roman builders and engineers, a 'benchmark' was a vital feature of any building project, the technology then being introduced to Britain. A benchmark was, and technically still is for that matter, a series of broad, arrow-shaped marks carved vertically into an existing stone building or large rock. A horizontal cut would then be added along the tip and an angle iron inserted to form a 'bench' upon which a level could be placed. The benchmark would act as a reference point for site surveyors for assessing the elevation of a building or surrounding area.

A **Bolt from the Blue** means a complete and unexpected surprise. The Romans termed a flash of lightning on a sunny day as a 'thunderbolt from the blue' and they would use this phrase figuratively to explain any kind of sudden surprise. The term became common parlance in the English-speaking world thanks to Thomas Carlyle's book *The French Revolution* (1837), which included the line: 'Arrestment, sudden really as a bolt from the blue, has hit strange victims.' The expression **Out of the Blue** is a simple variation of the idiom.

When something has **Bitten the Dust** it is worn out, broken down or even dead. The expression became widespread thanks to the American cowboy movies so popular in the early part of the 20th century. It is highly likely to have been picked up by US script-writers from a poem by the 19th-century sonneteer William Cullen Bryant which included the line: 'his fellow warriors, many a one, fall round him to the earth and bite the dust'. Although the phrase originally applied to warriors (or indeed cowboys) who died in battle, it is now frequently used to describe almost anything that is no longer any use to us. For example, your relationship with someone may have 'bitten the dust' and so might your old car or the new washing machine (good thing it's still under guarantee). The origin of the expression goes back a very long way – it is in fact one of our oldest idioms, even pre-dating the Bible by 850 years. While Psalm 72:9 gives us: 'They that dwell in the wilderness shall bow before him, and his enemies shall lick the dust', the source of the phrase can be found nearly three thousand years ago in the *Iliad*, written sometime in the eighth century BC. In the text, Homer describes the legend of the Trojan War and how soldiers fell dying with their faces in the dirt as though they were 'biting the dust'.

Living in Cloud Cuckoo Land means living as if in another world, separated from reality. The person in question is a bit of a dreamer, in other words. The phrase is an easy one to explain as it is actually a translation of the Greek 'Nephelococcygia' – an imaginary city built by cuckoos in the sky – from *The Birds*, a comedy written by Aristophanes in the 5th century BC.

If someone is **Blowing Hot and Cold** they are undecided and inconsistent in their actions. Generally speaking, they are hard to rely on as their views about a matter change repeatedly. The origin of this expression can be traced to a legend in Classical mythology of a traveller who was given food and shelter by a kindly satyr (a woodland god with the horns, tail and legs of a goat and an attendant of Bacchus, the god of wine and lustfulness). According

to the legend, the satyr gave the traveller a room for the night and some hot soup. The man blew on his fingers to warm them and then, with the same breath, blew on the soup to cool it. Irritated at the man's apparent indecision, the satyr packed him off outside and sent him back on his travels. (Sounds like the hotel I am staying in at the moment.)

Black Dog moods are periods of depression and sullen spirits. The expression was popularized during the 1930s and 1940s by Winston Churchill, who famously suffered from bouts of depression, which he called his 'black dogs'. However, the origin of the expression (which Churchill, being a well-educated man, would have known) dates back to a myth described by the Roman poet Horace which insists that the sight of a black dog and her puppies was an unlucky omen with grave consequences. For centuries, black dogs have been threatening symbols of folklore and superstition in different cultures. During the 1800s, for example, it became popular to use the expression 'a black dog has walked all over him/her' to describe a declining state of mental health.

A **Storm in a Tea Cup** is a petty argument or fight over nothing serious that is quickly resolved and soon forgotten. The Roman orator and statesman Cicero started it all off when he wrote '*excitabat fluctus in simpulo*', which, translated literally, means 'he whipped up waves in a ladle'. Other distinguished writers throughout history have followed suit, including the Duke of Ormond, who coined the phrase 'a storm in a cream bowl' in 1678; the Grand Duke Paul of Russia, with his 'tempest in a glass of water' from around 1790; and Lord Thurlow, who used the phrase 'storm in a wash hand basin' in 1830. It is easy to see how the previous expressions were adapted to include the nation's favourite afternoon drink (introduced to England in 1657 and quickly gaining in popularity). The expression passed into regular use thanks to a play, produced at the Garrick Theatre in London in 1936, entitled *A Storm in a Tea Cup*.

To be **Caught on the Horns of a Dilemma** is to be facing a choice of two equally unfavourable situations. The Greek word *lemma* may be loosely translated as 'expectation' or 'guess', and a 'dilemma' is a double *lemma*, or 'double problem'. Greek philosophers compared this to the two horns of a bull, which can both cause damage. If you choose to protect yourself from one horn, the other is still as much of a danger potentially.

To **Call a Spade a Spade** is an expression we frequently use to describe plain speaking or putting things bluntly. The phrase is over two thousand years old and can be traced to the ancient Greeks, who had a proverb to explain a person speaking their mind, which was to 'call figs figs and a tub a tub'. The Greek historian and philosopher Plutarch first recorded the phrase in *Sayings of Kings and Commanders*, but it was the Dutch humanist and scholar Erasmus who substituted the word 'spade' for the word 'tub'. In 1500, Erasmus published *Adagia*, his book of proverbs, and as a result the expression began to be widely used and has been popular ever since.

Once the **Die Has Been Cast** a chain of events has been started and there is no turning back; the deed is irreversible. The expression is credited to Julius Caesar, uttered when he sent his army across the Rubicon and into war with Rome. But, in fact, we can trace the words further back, to the year 300 BC, and a well-known Greek proverb that was discovered in the work of the philosopher Meander. Caesar, it turns out, was merely quoting the proverb. Meander's reference was to the game of dice, which was just about all they had to play with some 2,300 years ago. All dice games are based on chance, with very little skill required, and once the die has been rolled (cast) then the players must accept the outcome, whatever it may be. There is no going back to the beginning – an idea that Meander was paralleling in his philosophy.

*

If we are having a **Dog Day**, or a **Dog Day Afternoon**, then it is very hot, making us feel lazy and unable to exert ourselves in any way. This expression has nothing to do with our canine friends or their mating season, as some have suggested in the past. In fact it is an expression we can trace to the Romans and the days they called the *Canicularis Dies*, between 3 July and 11 August, when the dog star Sirius rises at the same time as the sun. According to the Romans, these were the hottest days of the year by far as they believed that the earth bore the combined heat of both Sirius and the sun at the same time. There are many other phrases using the word 'dog'. For example, **Doggone** is a favoured term from the American Bible Belt, used to express surprise and as a euphemistic alternative to 'God damn (it)', which wouldn't do at all for pious folk to utter. It derives from William Carleton's *Farm Ballads* (1873): 'But when that choir got up to sing, I couldn't catch a word,/They sang about the doggonest thing, a body ever heard.' A **Dog in a Manger** is someone who is not prepared to allow others to benefit from something that they themselves cannot use. The phrase relates to one of Aesop's fables, which tells us a tale about an ox and a dog who were stabled together for the night. Both were starving hungry and the only food available was the hay in the manger. Dogs do not eat hay but the ox was happily tucking in until the jealous hound began snapping and biting at him. The dog sat in the manger and would not allow the ox to eat, preferring instead to deprive his friend of the hay. (See also **Dog in the Night-time** and **In the Doghouse.**)

A **Draconian Measure** is considered a harsh and old-fashioned punishment, law or rule. The expression actually derives from the Draconian Code, which could be found in Athens in the seventh century BC at a time when the authorities appointed Draco to oversee law and order and apply punishment in the name of the state. Draco drew up a code of laws that were so severe that almost any crime at all was considered to be a capital offence, punishable by death. The orator Demandes famously claimed that Draco's code was actually 'written in the blood of criminals'.

If something **Fits to a T** then it is perfect for whatever purpose it is intended for; it fits precisely. All draughtsmen use a T-square for their work, to ensure perfect angles in their designs. However, the expression has been in existence since the late 1600s, long before the T-square became a common tool for architects and designers. In fact, the T stands for 'tittle', which comes from the medieval Latin word *titulus*, meaning 'tiny'. The 'tittle' is a very small brushstroke or pen mark positioned on a drawing and the term was first used in a figurative way in the 14th century by the religious reformer John Wycliffe, who used the word to describe the minute differences in his version of the New Testament. In this case, something that fits to a T is just about as accurate, and hence perfect, as the scribe's or draughtsman's tittle would be. Another associated expression is **I Don't Give a Jot or a Tittle**, which implies a person cares nothing at all about something. The phrase 'I don't give a jot' is thousands of years old and is identical to 'I don't give one iota'. The origins for both can be found in the early Greek language. A 'jot' is the letter 'iota', the smallest in the Greek alphabet. It was used at the time to imply 'the least of anything', and that is how the phrase became widely used for not caring in the slightest. Finally, we have the phrase **Tittle Tattle** that is used to describe any minor piece of gossip or news. *Tattle* is an Old English word for 'idle chat' or 'chatter', therefore to add the 'tittle' in front of 'tattle' reinforced the idea of very small talk.

To **Give the Thumbs Up** is a sign of approval, often given as a gesture, while **Thumbs Down** indicates disapproval. Both gestures are used throughout the world, regardless of language or culture, and their origin can be found in the Roman amphitheatres of two thousand years ago. If a gladiator found himself at the mercy of his opponent, he would look to the emperor for a thumbs-up gesture to show approval for his fighting skills. If the crowd were shouting '*mitte, mitte*', meaning 'let him go free', then a thumbs-up gesture would follow and he would be spared. At the very least he would hope to see a closed-hand gesture (*pollicem comprimere*) as an indication that he had fought well, but the thumbs in a downward position and the chant of '*lugula*' meant a horrible end for the poor chap in front of thousands of Romans baying for his blood.

Our **Halcyon Days** are those sun-filled, peaceful times we look back upon with affection and nostalgia. In other words, it was before you were married. *Halcyon* is the Greek word for 'kingfisher', coming from the word *hals*, meaning 'the sea', and *kuon*, translated as 'to conceive', and deriving in turn from the myth of the goddess Halkuon (or Halcyone), who collapsed in grief when her husband was drowned in a shipwreck. It was said that when the news of the tragedy reached her, she threw herself into the sea and also drowned. The gods were so touched by her romantic gesture that they brought them both back to life as kingfishers, who lived happily ever after on a floating nest. The gods also decreed that from that time onwards whenever the kingfishers were breeding in their sea nests, which was always during the 14-day period of the winter solstice, the waters would be kept calm and the wind still. They were the calm and tranquil winter days that became known as 'halcyon days'.

*

SHAGGY DOGS AND BLACK SHEEP

To **Let Bygones Be Bygones** is to forgive and forget without allowing past events to cloud our attitude in the future. This is a proverbial expression used in England since 1546, deriving from the Old English word *bygone*, meaning 'thing of the past'. The origin of the expression can be traced to around AD 20 and the Greek stoic philosopher and former slave Epictetus.

The **Lion's Share** is a phrase we have used since the late 18th century to describe the larger portion, the majority. It is likely this expression originates in an Aesop's fable dating to around 600 BC. The tale tells us how a lion, a fox and an ass went hunting and killed a stag, which the ass promptly divided into equal portions, but the lion looked upon this gesture as an insult to his pride and dignity, so he ate the ass. The fox was a little more cunning and ate just a small part, leaving the lion the largest share. The moral here is don't be an ass but be a little more fox-like and cunning instead. However, it is also a fact that the lion does naturally get the largest share of any kill brought to him by one of the lionesses in a pride.

The **Mob** is the name we give to a crowd of people who usually have violent intentions. The expression, in use since the days of the Roman empire, stems from the Latin phrase *mobile vulgus*, meaning 'unruly crowd'. By the mid 17th century, the opinions of ordinary people in England began to be voiced and such crowds were regarded as 'mobiles', later shortened to the 'mobs' we all know and fear today.

Winning the Plaudits is to be receiving acclaim or approval of those whom you seek to impress. In use in England since the 1600s, the root of the expression is Latin, from the word *plaudite* ('applaud') that was traditionally shouted out by Roman actors at the end of each performance to indicate to the audience the show had ended. Therefore an actor or actress on the receiving end of 'plaudits' was highly appreciated by those he or she had been entertaining.

BOTH SIDES OF THE LAW

The phrase **Red Tape** suggests officious formality, or regulations being adhered to with rigid excess, usually slowing down decision-making or other transactions, typically in business. For centuries all legal and government documents have been bound with a red ribbon. An advert placed in *Public Intelligence*, a public service newspaper, on 6 December 1658 – in which a reward was offered for 'a small bundle of papers tied with a red tape which was lost on Friday last' – provides the earliest evidence of this. In Victorian times, administrators for the British Raj in India tied all their documents with red tape and these would be moved around by 'peons' (office boys), who were generally slow, badly organized and often misplaced the files altogether. Which sounds not unlike the average office found anywhere in the service sector these days.

It was Charles Dickens who popularized the phrase

and ensured its regular use. Before writing novels, Dickens was a parliamentary sketch writer nicknamed 'Boz'. From the House of Commons, Boz would report on each day's proceedings, all of which were bound with red tape once business was concluded, and he often used the phrase in his articles. In his novel *Bleak House* (1852–3), Dickens attacks the abuses of the Court of Chancery and satirizes what he terms government 'red tape'. The expression also appears in others of his books, including *The Old Curiosity Shop* (1840–41) and *Little Dorrit* (1855–7). During an interview in the 1860s, Dickens was quoted as saying: 'I wrote three anti-Tory verses for the *Examiner* after the general election in 1841, and I invented the Circumlocution Office in *Little Dorrit* as an attack on the scandalous red tape with which the Crimean War was mismanaged.'

To put on your **Thinking Cap** is to take time to consider a problem and hopefully solve it. In the very early law courts, it became traditional for a judge to wear a black cap to show the court he had heard all the evidence he needed in order to reach a decision. It was a signal that he was now in the process of considering his verdict and would soon be passing sentence. In later years, this practice was restricted to the passing of a death sentence only, but in either case this was the original 'thinking cap'.

To have a **Skeleton in the Cupboard** is to have a shameful secret hidden away. I remember once as a

small boy asking my mother, after watching a programme about missing siblings, if I had any brothers
or sisters I didn't know about. She told me we didn't
have any 'skeletons like that in our cupboards', which
needless to say scared the life out of me as I wondered how many children had been locked up for
ever in cupboards for being naughty. It is certainly
possible that the actual discovery of a skeleton in a
cupboard may provide the origin of the phrase, but
it is more likely to come from the study of human
anatomy. Up until 1832, it was illegal to dissect a
human body for the benefit of medical research, but
of course many a physician still did, leading to suggestions that they hid their skeletons in surgery cupboards. It is also true that after the dissecting of
bodies became legal, grave robbers would dig up
newly buried corpses and sell them to unscrupulous
doctors in an underhand way. This practice was so
frowned upon that the medical men would try to
keep their secrets hidden away in locked cupboards.
The phrase first appeared in print in 1845 in an article
in *Punch*, written by the novelist William Makepeace
Thackeray, and again in his book *The Newcomes*
(1855), which includes the line: 'And it is from these
that we shall arrive at some particulars regarding
the Newcomes family, which will show us that they
have a skeleton or two in their closets as well as their
neighbours.' It has been part of the English language
ever since. To this day, my parents probably still
wonder where the keys to all the wardrobes in our

house went. (Still over the fence behind next door's shed, I should imagine.)

To do a **Moonlight Flit** is to take leave without notice or permission and to move on to another place. The word *flit* is an Old English and Scottish word, meaning 'to move house', which derives in turn from the Norse word *flytja* and which has been in use since the Middle Ages. Between then and the 1930s, it was common for people to disappear quickly from their lodgings under cover of darkness, leaving bills unpaid and using only the moonlight to find their way to a new town and place to live. By contrast, nothing could be worse for a tenant than to do a 'flit' on a cloudy night, walking around in circles for hours, only to be found curled up on their landlord's doorstep at dawn the next day. From the late 19th until the early 20th century, it was fashionable to use the phrase 'shooting the moon' instead, which is illustrated by Sir Walter Besant in his novel *All Sorts and Conditions of Men* (1882): 'I told him who were responsible tenants and I warned him when shootings of the moon seemed likely.' In *Down and Out in Paris and London* (1933), George Orwell confirms the expression was still in regular use some 50 years later: 'I remember how surprised she was at my asking instead of removing the clothes on the sly as shooting the moon was a common trick in our quarter.'

A related expression that also brings illegal nocturnal activities to mind is **Moonshine**. In America

this indicates 'empty
words' or 'nonsense', alluding no
doubt to the transient, insubstantial quality of
moonlight. The word was also applied to contra-
band alcohol made by 'moonshiners' during the
Prohibition years of the 1920s, and conjures up
images of alcohol being illegally made and distributed under the cover of darkness, although that use
of the word originally dates to the 1700s and the
illegal practice of smuggling French brandy into
England during the night. The brandy in question
was also codenamed 'moonshine' by smugglers.
Finally, we have **Moonlighting**, a phrase commonly
applied to anybody carrying out a second job, usually at night, to earn extra money that is not declared
to the authorities, in the hope of avoiding tax.

A **Nonce** is a prison slang term for a sex offender.

Such characters are kept separately from other prisoners to avoid the possibility of violent attack. However, in Victorian times these offenders were housed in the same prison wings and usually on the same landings as the rest of the inmates, but would only be let out of their cells when the others were safely locked up. To ensure no mistakes were made, prison officials would chalk the letters N-O-N-C-E above their cell doors, standing for 'Not On Normal Courtyard Exercise'. There is also a suggestion that this phrase was reinforced by the expression 'He's in prison for a little bit of nonsense'.

London police constables have been nicknamed **Bobbies** since they first patrolled the streets in the 1830s. The nickname came about as a reference to Sir Robert Peel (1788–1850), who founded the original police force. At the time they were also known as 'Peelers Men', or just plain 'Peelers', but that is a nickname very rarely used these days. In polite circles, they are known as **Constables**, a term that can be traced back to the Middle Ages when the governors of the royal castles were called 'constables'. The word is derived from the Old French word *conestable*, which in turn comes from the Latin *comes stabuli*, translated as 'count of the stable' (head officer). The word **Constabulary** was first recorded in the late 15th century when it officially denoted the district under the responsibility of a certain constable. There is also the word **Cop** or **Copper** – mostly used in

America – that some researchers have suggested stands for 'Constable On Patrol'. Some Americans even insist the word has its roots in the copper badges the first New York patrolmen wore, which were actually made of brass and silver. The word in fact originated in medieval England and is a variation of the word 'cap', meaning 'to arrest', which in turn derives from the Old French word *caper*, meaning 'to seize', from the Latin *capere* ('to take'). That is also where we find the origins of expressions such as 'cop a load of that' and 'he's copped one straight on the head'.

To **Double Cross** a person (or to be 'double crossed') is to cheat somebody, or to betray a confidence. Initially this phrase used to indicate that both parties were involved in the deception, although it is now commonly understood as applying to only one party. There is a suggestion that this expression began life in the Middle Ages when Venetian merchants (Venice being the capital of the trading world at that time) would affect allegiance to fellow Westerners by making the sign of the cross in the way Westerners did, and then show the same loyalty to Easterners by crossing themselves in the way Easterners used to. It is said that this divided loyalty led to the introduction of the term 'double crosser'. But there is stronger evidence suggesting the expression is far more recent, being in fact a horse-racing term from the early 19th century. Any jockey who had been paid to lose an event by race fixers, but who then found himself in the lead, would cross himself twice as he passed the winning post as a prayer to God for forgiveness for his double deception by accepting the bribe to lose and then winning the race. He might also have added a third cross to pray the race fixers weren't waiting for him when he got home for his tea.

Another possible origin for the term, and one that I prefer, relates to the doings of an 18th-century bounty hunter by the name of Jonathan Wilde. Legend has it that Wilde kept a book with the names listed of all the criminals and wanted men throughout England. He formed an underground information network and would pay or protect any criminal who provided him with information on the whereabouts of another. In this way, Wilde would apprehend and turn over wanted men to the authorities for a fee. Each of these informers had a cross placed next to their name in the book of thieves. Once a man was no longer useful to Wilde, or began to refuse to give information, the Thief Taker General would place a second cross against his name and then turn him in for the bounty money. However, Wilde also used to blackmail men to steal for him and even to murder rivals, so inevitably he was eventually double crossed himself, turned in and hanged for his crimes.

A **Hatchet Job** is usually a brutal and unpleasant task carried out by **Hatchet Men**. This may take the form of mass redundancies or even the closure of various places of work, for the financial benefit of a few investors. The origins of both expressions can be found in the American gang warfare of the 1920s. When the Chinese drug gangs began arriving in US cities, Chinese gang leaders and outwardly respectable businessmen would sometimes hire a man with a hatchet to murder rivals. The expression 'hatchet men' was later applied to hired gunmen and extended into commerce, followed inevitably by politics and journalism, where it is still used as a term to describe anybody hired to destroy someone's reputation or credibility. I don't think I will be making any jokes about any of them. The word 'hatchet' derives from the old French word *hachette*, meaning 'small axe', an extension of the word *hache*, which is an axe.

A **Man of Straw** is the front man of an enterprise who appears to be in a position of authority but is in fact controlled by others who are less visible but who hold the real power. In modern times they are more likely to be thought of as puppets or figureheads. The expression can be traced to the law courts and the dubious practice of men and women who would attend court each day in the hope they would be employed by lawyers and swear on oath anything that was asked of them, in return for a fee. They would sit around waiting for lawyers to call for them and could be identified by the straw they stuffed into their shoes. Many a case, between the 16th and 19th centuries, would be decided on evidence given by the 'straw men', also termed 'straw dolls'. By 1811, the expression had passed into wider use and labourers would look for work with straw placed in their shoes, both for comfort and to indicate they were available for hire.

Since the 1940s, **Porridge** has been used as a slang term for prison. The term has been in use in England since the 1500s and referred originally to a soup thickened with barley, the word deriving from the Old French *potage*, meaning 'soup' or (literally) 'that which is put into the pot'. There are several suggestions for how 'porridge' came to mean 'prison', the first being the Anglo-Saxon word *styr*, meaning 'punishment' (the connection being that you have to 'stir' porridge constantly while cooking it, but also where 'stir', as a slang word for prison, comes from). There is also the theory that porridge was once a prisoner's basic food. Between 1974 and 1979, *Porridge*, starring Ronnie Barker and Richard Beckinsale as prisoners sharing a cell, was one of the most popular comedy shows on British television, the lead character (played by Barker) being a wily Londoner who used cockney rhyming slang. And it is rhyming slang that leads us to the most likely source of the word, in my view. Since the mid 1800s, the phrase 'borage and thyme' has been used to mean 'time', which in turn was the word convicts used to describe a jail sentence. Could the root be a simple transformation over the years of 'borage' to 'porridge'?

LOVE AND DEATH

Wearing Your Heart on Your Sleeve is a phrase used to describe someone who is prepared to show their affection openly and obviously. During the Middle

Ages, and the great tournaments where noble knights battled for honour and prestige, it was common for a lady to 'give her heart' to a knight at such occasions in the form of a handkerchief or other token of affection. The knight would then enter the lists with the lady's 'heart' pinned to his sleeve, for all the spectators to see.

The **Bridegroom** is the lucky chap who gets to spend months and months working out seating plans and menus and a thousand other vitally important details, which, come the big day, nobody even notices anyway (or none of the male guests do, at any rate). All in all, being the bridegroom is a thankless business. In fact, the only interesting thing about the whole mad event is how the word 'bridegroom' came about in the first place. The Old English word for a man marrying his sweetheart is *brydguma*, which literally means 'bride man'. However, over the years the word *guma*, meaning 'man', has become confused with the word 'groom', which meant 'manservant'. Which is largely what the poor chap has become anyway. 'I now pronounce you bride and manservant.' (That sounds about right, doesn't it?)

These days a **Honeymoon** is the holiday that newly married couples take directly after their wedding. The expression is also applied to the period a person is given to settle into a new job or role before they are expected to produce positive results. There are two suggestions for the origin of this word. The first takes us back to ancient Egypt where it was customary for a bride's father to provide his new son-in-law with all the mead he could drink for the period of one month. Mead is a type of wine made from honey and so that month (the period between one full moon and the next) was called the 'honeymoon' (literally 'honey month').

The second suggestion is far more recent and rooted in Europe. It was an ancient custom for all newly married couples to share a drink of diluted honey, during the first month of their marriage, to reinforce the 'sweetness' of those early weeks together. The phrase was in regular use by 1546 and described by Dr Johnson in his *Dictionary of the English Language* (first published on 17 April 1755, having taken eight years to complete) as 'the first month after marriage when there is nothing but tenderness and pleasure'. Either way, the one thing you can be sure of is that it will never last.

A **Tomboy** is a young girl who behaves more as a boy might do. It is an expression that can be traced back to the 16th century. The word derives from the old Anglo-Saxon word *tumbere*, which means 'dancer' or 'romper', and is from the same root at the French word *tomber*, which means 'to fall' or 'tumble', and which also gave us 'tom rig', a 17th-century term for a prostitute or 'loose woman'. ('Rig' came about from the French word *rigoler*, meaning 'to make merry'). Meanwhile, in Australia the phrase 'tom tart' was regularly used to describe a lady, possibly as a result of cockney rhyming slang (tom tart = sweetheart), and in America the expression 'tommy' meant 'romping girl'. Back in England, the good old cockney rhyming slang came up with 'tommy tucker' as a term for a loose woman. (I'll leave you to guess what that rhymes with.) It is thus easy to see how the current slang term 'tom', for 'prostitute', has evolved.

Any person **Shilly Shallying** around is known to be undecided and hesitant about something or someone. During the Middle Ages, a well-known phrase expressing uncertainty was 'shall I, shall I'. By the 17th century this had evolved into 'to go shill I, shall I' – an easy step to 'shilly shally'. A variation on the theme is **Dilly Dally** – a simple play on the word 'dally', meaning to linger or dawdle – as is the expression **Willy Nilly**, indicating an action that will take place with or without the consent of the person on the receiving end (originally 'will he, nill he', followed by 'will ye, nill ye' and finally settling into 'will I, nill I').

*

A child born **On the Wrong Side of the Blanket** is born outside wedlock and hence illegitimate. This is a delicate reference to the offspring resulting from illicit and hurried sexual encounters, which would often take place on top of a bed instead of inside it. At least that was the way it was seen in the 18th century when Tobias Smollett wrote in his book *The Expedition of Humphry Clinker* (1771): 'My mother was an honest woman. I didn't come in on the wrong side of the blanket.' I wonder what Smollett would have written if he were alive today: 'My mother was an honest woman. I didn't come in on the back seat of an old Vauxhall Nova'?

A **Bunny Boiler** is a former lover, always female, who refuses to accept a relationship is over and will go to any lengths to make her man pay dearly for the rejection. She is an unhinged and dangerous woman. The expression originates from the film *Fatal Attraction* (1987), starring Michael Douglas and Glenn Close. Dan (played by Douglas) is a happily married man, but embarks on a torrid affair with Alex (Glenn Close), then abruptly ends the liaison as soon as he has had his fill. But Alex does not handle this rejection well and begins a vicious campaign of revenge, culminating with Dan returning home to find his daughter's pet rabbit boiling in water on the kitchen stove. For the bunny huggers among you, don't worry – it wasn't a real rabbit. Now let me entertain you with a few tales of some real-life 'bunny boilers'.

One wronged young lady who had been cheated on and then dumped repaid her former lover by letting herself into his flat on the day he went off on a week's holiday with his new girlfriend. While there she dialled the speaking clock in New York and set the receiver down on the table. She then spooned fish guts into his boiler, sprinkled watercress seeds all over his furniture and carpets, watered them and then turned the boiler up to full heat before leaving and letting nature take its course.

Others have emailed intimate photographs to work colleagues and friends after editing them on a computer programme to include animals, fetish equipment and reduce the size of certain parts. Some have smeared dog faeces thinly under desks and chairs so that it cannot be found, but certainly smelt, and there are stories of run-over pets, smashed-up cars and broken windows. But my favourite is the story of the girl who went back to her ex to 'plead' for reconciliation. The poor fellow saw this as an opportunity to take advantage of the girl's vulnerable state and initiated, in his mind at least, 'one last' sexual encounter. But our heroine had come prepared and after handcuffing him to the bed (part of their normal routine) she then applied make-up on him, dressed him in a nappy, put one of the most outrageous DVDs the local shop could find (which featured bestiality) into the player and then phoned the hapless chap's mother and father, who lived just one road away, telling them that he badly needed their help. With that, she dressed herself, waved goodbye and left the front door open as she went, passing his mother and father as they hurried round to see what the problem was. Gentlemen, you have been warned!

To **Lead Someone Up the Garden Path** is to mislead a person completely. The expression has been in regular use since the early 1900s, and probably refers to the place where a seduction could be carried out, in those stiff Victorian days, after the promise of marriage. On country estates throughout England, footpaths criss-cross the acres of garden, often leading to summerhouses or follies tucked away from the main residence. This is traditionally where a gentleman would propose marriage to a young lady. Indeed, it was at one such place, the Temple of Diana in the gardens of Blenheim Palace, during the summer of 1908, that that great English gentleman Sir Winston Churchill (the greatest Englishman of all time, according to a recent TV poll) proposed to Clementine Hozier, who became his devoted wife. However, some gentlemen would lead a pretty maiden to such a place not to propose, but to introduce the rest of himself to the young lady. The scoundrel – he should be horsewhipped at once!

To **Give Someone the Willies** is to arouse unease and fear in them. The willies can make some people quite nervous, you know. (Come off it, girls, it's not that funny!) The source of this expression is unclear but in bygone days a willow tree was called a 'willy'. The weeping 'willy' tree (called 'weeping' because of its long trailing branches resembling streams of tears) has long been associated with grief and mourning and English literature is littered with examples such as 'at that time he was in his willies' in reference to a widower. In the 19th-century ballet *Giselle*, the eponymous heroine is possessed by the Wilis – the ghosts of beautiful young girls who had died just before their wedding day. The souls dance to express their anger at missing out on their biggest day. These days the idiom is more likely to relate to nerves or apprehension than to grief.

A **Dead Ringer** is a well-known phrase for somebody who looks just like another. In medieval Britain, the medical profession was not quite as refined as it is now, and people could be pronounced dead, when they may have simply been unconscious. (And this was also before comas were fully understood.) It was not uncommon for bodies to be later exhumed by body snatchers, and corpses might be found with their fingers worn to the bone, a clear indication they had returned to life and tried to claw their way out of their coffins. So horrific was this image that the English gentry began mistrusting medical opinion and in some cases would bury their loved ones with a string attached to their wrists connected to a bell above the grave. Anybody who returned to life and found themselves prematurely buried could attract attention by ringing the bell, and it has been recorded that this actually worked. Many 'bodies' were exhumed after bells were rung and some people carried on with their lives as before. But when they were spotted in the street, startled acquaintances might exclaim to each other: 'That looks just like Jack Jones! I thought he was dead.' To which they would receive the reply: 'Yes, he must be a dead ringer.' And that, believe it or not, is true.

To have **Kicked the Bucket** is an expression used to describe the dearly departed, those no longer of this world, the deceased. There are three possible explanations for the phrase and the squeamish should cover their eyes while reading, or look away now. The first relates to abattoirs and slaughterhouses where culled animals would be hung by the hind legs from an overhead beam, called a 'bucket', while blood drained from the carcass into a tin bucket below. Any twitching or spasms would result in the poor creature kicking one of the buckets. The word for the overhead beam derives from the Old French word *buquet*, meaning 'balance'. The second explanation is provided by the lynch mobs (see **Lynch Mob**) and their method of standing a victim on an upturned pail, or bucket, placed under a tree while securing a noose to an overhead branch. Kicking the bucket away would then deliver justice, lynch-mob style. Suicide is our third option and an article published in the *London Magazine* during 1823, by Thomas De Quincy, provides a description: 'One Bolsover, having hung himself to a beam, while standing on the bottom of a bucket, kicked the vessel away in order to pry into futurity and it was all up with him from that instant – finis!'

The **Guillotine** was a method of execution used widely during the French Revolution. Invented by Dr Antoine Louis (1723–92), the machine was originally called a 'Louison' or 'Louisette' and first used in Italy during the mid 1700s. But it was Dr Joseph-Ignace Guillotin (1738–1814) who pushed a resolution through the French Assembly in 1792 adopting the Louison as the official 'painless and humane' method of executing criminals. The newly named guillotine (the 'e' making it a feminine derivative) became immediately famous when it cut the French aristocracy down to size during 'La Terreur' the following year (see **The Baker**). However, Guillotin's family were so unhappy at being associated with such a device that, after his death, they changed their name and from then onwards lived anonymously.

Thomas Carlyle wrote in *The French Revolution* (1838): 'Which product popular gratitude or levity christens by a feminine derivative name, as if it were his daughter; La Guillotine! . . . Unfortunate Doctor! For twenty two years he, unguillotined himself, shall hear nothing but guillotine, see nothing but guillotine and his name will outlive Caesar's.' These days, a 'guillotine' indicates a far less sinister device – for cutting paper or for use in surgery.

INDEX OF THE WORDS
AND PHRASES

INDEX OF THE WORDS AND PHRASES

INDEX OF THE WORDS AND PHRASES